# Literary Gardens

# Literary Gardens

## The Imaginary Gardens of Writers and Poets

Sandra Lawrence

Illustrations by
Lucille Clerc

# Contents

# Introduction

*'She held back the swinging curtain of ivy and pushed back the door...'*

*The Secret Garden*, Frances Hodgson Burnett, 1911

Mention the phrase 'gardens in literature' and, almost without exception, one book will spring to mind. Frances Hodgson Burnett's childhood classic *The Secret Garden* was not the first novel to channel the mystery and romance of plants in expressing a melancholy for something lost, but its themes of redemption live so profoundly in the human soul it haunts even people who claim not to have read it.

A garden spoken about in the past tense always carries the poignance of something that once was and is now gone. A disproportionate number of novels about gardens are intimately entwined with the pains of growing up, as with Philippa Pearce's *Tom's Midnight Garden* or Giorgio Bassani's *The Garden of the Finzi-Continis*. The veiled brutality of the heroine's loss of innocence in Sandra Cisneros's *The House on Mango Street* is all the more shocking for its leafy setting. Other literary gardens press the different but equally tender bruises of missed opportunity. As a child, the sheer wealth of possibility everywhere one looks, naturally means that some of those possibilities will be missed, only to be regretted years later.

It is particularly joyful, then, to read books that celebrate the garden for nothing more than the delight one can find there. Elizabeth von Arnim's *Elizabeth and her German Garden*, for example, has been adored for its sheer joie de vivre ever since publication in 1898. Then there are the gardens of almost unfathomable mystery, such as in Vivant Denon's *No Tomorrow* and Jorge Luis Borge's bizarre 'The Garden of Forking Paths'. Like the two children in Italo Calvino's 'The Enchanted Garden' we are compelled to explore the forbidden, but fearful of what we might find.

Comic gardens are comparatively rare. Such spaces are too important, too filled with emotion to be treated so lightly. In the rare instances that they provide a backdrop for comedy, as in Oscar Wilde's *The Importance of Being Earnest* or Terry Pratchett's Discworld series, they often *acquire* poignance as our own twenty-twenty hindsight kicks in. We know what happened to Wilde shortly after his final play opened; Pratchett himself was only too aware of growing ever closer to his recurring dark gardener.

For space reasons I tried to set a few boundaries. Alas, I couldn't even stay within my own simple rules. 'No poetry,' I told myself, yet the *Rāmāyaṇa*, one of my favourite epic poems, was a deal-breaker. In it went. My 'no non-fiction' red line was crossed by the beauty of Jamaica Kincaid's love for all gardens. Similarly, I had determined to leave out plays, mainly because I couldn't decide which Shakespearian gardens to omit. As I sent packing the Capulet mansion, however, even as Sir Toby Belch's box-tree hiding place disappeared, as Ophelia's bouquet was benched and Perdita's grassy bank joined the substitute list, Oscar Wilde sneaked back in under the red line, cocking a merry snook at best-laid plans.

In a book such as this, much like those 'Top 100' lists so popular in magazines and on the internet, no individual's choice can ever meet universal approval. I promise that *everyone* who reads this book will grind their teeth due to at least one or two scandalously obvious omissions. Even I don't approve of my own choices. Or rather, I berate myself for the gardens I had to leave out, some of which were on the list from the very start but fell by the flower-strewn wayside as word-count caught up with me. Just as I overfill my own garden with horticultural goodies impulse-purchased at the little sales point of potted-up seedlings at the end of a garden visit, I quickly overstuffed my brief with books; there was simply no more room. I wanted a range, both geographically and thematically, which meant that dear friends had to make way for new favourites.

My own childhood 'gateway drug' – the ruined formal garden in Enid Blyton's *The Treasure Hunters* – was first for the chop. Hemingford Grey Manor, better known as the eponymous *Green Knowe*, was another painful loss. Lauded as England's oldest continuously habited dwelling, the manor's garden remains almost exactly as it was when Lucy M. Boston described it, with its chessboard topiary, stone giant and mysterious woodlands. Equally, I mourned Boccaccio's perfumed retreat from the ravages of plague, an idyllic setting for youth and love and tales of romance in the *Decameron*. I was forced to drop Hildegard of Bingen's monastic herb garden because I found it hard to pinpoint specific descriptions within her writings, but I have no such excuse for the heartbreaking loss of Alain-Fournier's mysterious broken garden of *Le Grand Meaulnes*. I am equally disappointed not to have included the Owen Garden of Alice Hoffman's *Practical Magic*, along with a whole slew of gardens of the *Lost*, *Rose* and *Bone* varieties by Helen Humphreys, Susanna Kearsley and Tess Gerritsen respectively. John le Carré, Rumer Godden, Elizabeth Gilbert, J.G. Ballard, Henry James and Jean Giono, I apologize to you all.

The yearning to experience a place that has touched the soul, in the way that only gardens in literature can, is so strong that where there is any chance at all – perhaps an author has based a garden on a real place or their home, or there is somewhere very similar in real life – I have included it in a *Visiting* section on page 186. I cannot, however, suggest real-world locations for most of the novels here, and nor would I want to. The whole point of gardens in literature is that is exactly where they are. They were created in the imagination and that is where they should stay.

# Misselthwaite Manor

## *The Secret Garden*
## Frances Hodgson Burnett, 1911

*'There's naught as nice as th' smell o' good earth'*

There are certain children's classics that linger in the imagination as a series of romantic moments, rather than being admired as a whole. The imagery in *The Secret Garden* is so heady, its ending so powerful, that it is easy to forget that in order to achieve redemption, transgression must occur. Some even claim the young heroine of Frances Hodgson Burnett's most enduring work is so very loathsome in the early chapters that they cannot bring themselves to read the rest of the novel.

Certainly, those very first pages are a tough read. Mary Lennox is a profoundly unpleasant individual, selfish, rude, even physically violent towards her Indian servants. Indeed, the very idea of Indian servants today leaves a sour taste in our post-colonial mouths. Burnett gives us reasons for Mary's strange, detached nature but not excuses, and while she seems exaggeratedly nasty to our modern eyes, we can rest assured she would have been deeply disagreeable to pre-First World War readers too.

Clutching at straws, the reader latches onto Mary's love of books. Surely no one who likes books can be all bad? We see her alone, retreated into herself, aloof, trying to make a flowerbed in the dirt, decorated with flowers. Then the tiny bubble of sympathy is burst by Mary's sickening musings on how best to hurt her clearly Muslim ayah. We watch her orphaned, taunted by other children, carted off to England to live with an obscure uncle, yet we remain as unmoved as she appears to be.

The characters continue unsympathetic. Dour Mrs Medlock the housekeeper informs Mary that her grim Uncle Archibald Craven does not want to see her. Mrs Craven, a possible ray of hope, is quickly dismissed as dead. The surrounding moors seem equally bleak and when Mary reaches the forbidding Misselthwaite Manor, she is ordered not to go poking around the gloomy old house. Burnett has provided us with the perfect nadir; now she must begin the uphill task of making us actually like her heroine.

The Yorkshire location is powerful, but not immediately obvious given Burnett's background. Although born in Manchester, England, her father died in 1853 when she was four, sending the family into a downward spiral ultimately resulting in emigration to the USA, where they scratched a living in a Tennessee cabin. Frances started writing to make money, publishing prolifically in magazines and books. She made her name with *Little Lord Fauntleroy*, which sold by the million, engendering shows on Broadway and London's West End, and making a fortune for purveyors of curling tongs and velvet suits.

After the death of one of her sons aged 16 and the failure of her first marriage, Burnett returned to England and rented the property best associated with her, Great Maytham in Kent. There, she began to restore the neglected garden which had captured her heart. It is often suggested the estate was the inspiration for *The Secret Garden*, but even taking into account its later Edwin Lutyens and Gertrude Jekyll remodelling (where the entrance to 'the secret garden' was bricked up) it is hard to shoehorn

the description of Misselthwaite into Great Maytham. Parts of it work, the old orchards and neglected fruit trees, for example, but in other respects Burnett's imagined paradise is exactly that: an invention.

Yorkshire is important to the book, and not just in the younger characters' constant attempts to master the dialect. The wind is always 'wuthering', bringing to mind another possible inspiration from one Emily Brontë, but Burnett only visited the county once. Years later, a remembered visit to the derelict hall at Fryston near Castleford may have sparked something in her.

Misselthwaite Manor stands, bleak, on Missel Moor ('thwaite' being old Norse for a clearing). Mary Lennox will meet a 'missel'[sic] thrush, named for its penchant for mistletoe berries, but it is another bird that perhaps gives us our clearest insight into Hodgson Burnett's inspirations.

Mary is at her loneliest ebb when she meets her first real friend, a robin. While *The Secret Garden* was not written until 1909, the bird is a reference to a difficult time in Burnett's own life. Newly divorced, bereaved of her oldest son, worried for the health of her second and reeling from a disastrous second marriage, she would later write a short memoir, *My Robin*, in which she describes one of her most important relationships, with a redbreast she encountered in the garden at Maytham. It reads like the first encounter with a lover. 'From that moment we never doubted each other for one second,' she writes. 'He knew and I knew'. Just as Mary's little robin shows her the key to her secret garden and accompanies her inside, but only on his terms, Burnett tells us: 'I did not own the robin – he owned me – or perhaps we owned each other'.

Mary is already beginning to thaw when she discovers the garden, stunned into a new consideration of servants by the cheery, no-nonsense Martha and gruff Ben Weatherstaff. That new consideration is of its time, of course, a romantic ideal of rosy-cheeked peasants living twelve-to-a-cottage under the loving gaze of an earth mother, but in Edwardian eyes, that is progress for a 'spoilt' child. 'How does tha' like thyself?' asks Martha. 'Not at all – really,' Mary replies, 'But I never really thought of that before'. Her honesty allows her to move on, to find a key – both literal and metaphorical – to potential happiness and friendship.

Our first, lingering impression of the garden's planting is oppressive: long strands of dark, overgrown ivy. A lover of gardens herself, Burnett

## Just being close to the secret garden, however, is enough to begin to heal Mary Lennox

knew what ten years' worth of ivy looks like. The secret garden's walls are so thick with it that the door is entirely concealed, even in the depths of winter. Just being close to the secret garden, however, is enough to begin to heal Mary Lennox. She is skipping with a rope for the first time ever, embodying the Edwardian ideal of fresh air and exercise as a cure-all; the sun is shining, the wind is blowing. Just as the robin has led Mary to the key, the breeze reveals the door. Winter has turned a corner.

She is entranced, but she does not yet understand what she has found. She sniffs the air and revels in the overgrown silence, and we luxuriate with her in 'this hazy tangle from tree to tree which made it all look so mysterious'. She is beginning to merit her reward, to make things grow, but she is not yet ready to receive it all. A haunting sense of melancholy is not yet dispelled. Mary learns that the lost Mrs Craven made the garden, that she loved it, and that it killed her. At the same time a second mystery is brewing, via strange cries heard at night inside the house.

How much of the garden is dead? Mary cannot tell, but someone can. The delightful Dickon is almost otherworldly, a wood-sprite sitting on a metaphorical tree stump within the great Victorian/Edwardian literary fashion for representations of the god Pan. Arthur Machen, Kenneth Grahame, Saki and J.M. Barrie all created romantic 'nature-boys' during this period, Dickon is just one of many, and much less sinister than some. His affinity with animals and all things that grow is the opposite of everything Mary has ever known. It is Dickon who helps Mary to her redemption, who explains what the strange spikes poking through the soil

really are: the first murmurings of spring. 'There's naught as nice as th' smell o' good earth,' he tells her, 'except th' smell o' fresh growing things when th' rain falls on 'em'.

Haunted by Martha's stories of Mrs Craven's roses, of 'gold coloured gorse blossoms an' th' blossoms o' the broom an' th' heather flowerin', all purple bells,' Mary wants the garden to live again, but on two conditions. It must not be like 'a gardener's garden' (was Burnett a disciple of William Robinson's 'wild' style of gardening?) and, even more importantly, it must remain a secret until the moment is right.

So potent are the garden's healing powers that they begin to work as far away as the gloom of the house. The equally obnoxious Colin visibly calms from his high-Victorian disease of 'hysteria' at the very mention of it. It cannot be just any garden – he threw a fit when he was taken into the manor's formal grounds – it must be the realm beyond the secret door. Having lived his entire life under the belief that he might die at any moment, he begins to hope. If he could only see the garden, he might have a chance at growing up. As his wheelchair approaches the high wall, he wavers. 'I can see nothing,' he whispers, 'There is no door'. Once again, it is the robin that shows the way, Mary and Dickon are merely conduits to Colin's wonder. 'I shall get well,' he cries, 'I shall live forever and ever and ever!'

Burnett charts the emotional growth of the two children through the slow change of the seasons: 'every day and every night it seemed as if Magicians were passing through it drawing loveliness out of the earth'.

Only Dickon remains constant; we get the feeling that he has always been as he is, and always will be. And here, once again, many modern readers cannot completely surrender to the romance of this ultimate healing garden. We are never far away from the difficult imagery of children ordering around forelock-tugging servants and discussing the servility of 'native' Indian staff. This is not something that would have bothered Burnett's readers. We cannot escape modern filters, we can only acknowledge that the past is, indeed, a different country.

As the novel continues, Burnett refers increasingly to the idea of 'magic' being worked by the garden. While she strongly implies that the enchantment is merely the will of the children to enact change, by blurring the edges between reality and magic, she keeps afloat the mysterious cloud of romance that has clung to the book since its publication. Does Archibald Craven's dead wife really whisper 'Come into the garden' during his long, lonely trek across Europe? Is the garden calling him? Can he sense the returning strength of his deeply damaged son in the clouds of blue forget-me-nots that haunt his dreams? Or is it just the pangs of a slowly mending heart? As he sees for himself the 'wilderness of autumn gold and purple and violet blue and flaming scarlet', as he witnesses the sheaves of late lilies, late roses and yellowing trees, he feels he has entered 'an embowered temple of gold'. 'I thought it would be dead,' he admits.

However we choose to read the book's climax, we will likely feel moved, as it appears Frances Hodgson Burnett herself was. She had

## So potent are the garden's healing powers that they begin to work as far away as the gloom of the house

adored Great Maytham, especially the old orchard. A hands-on gardener, she had planted more than three hundred roses, but she was only ever a tenant there. In 1907 the owner sold up and she had to leave, returning to America to be near her remaining son. She wrote *The Secret Garden* in 1909, and it was published across ten issues of *The American Magazine*, 1910–11. It was published as a novel in 1911, with dreamlike illustrations by Charles Robinson.

Burnett's original notes are lost, donated to a Manhattan school and long-since disappeared. We are forced once again to turn to her other 'garden' work to understand the true emotions behind the haunting melancholy even in the happiest moments of her most famous novel. In *My Robin*, Burnett talks of her distress at leaving Great Maytham, revealing that she went to explain to her friend why she was leaving him. 'You must not think when I do not come back it is because I have forgotten you,' she tells the little bird. 'We won't say Goodbye. We have been too near to each other – nearer than human beings are. I love you and love you and love you – little Soul'.

'Then I went out of the rose-garden. I shall never go into it again.'

# Manderley

## *Rebecca*
## Daphne du Maurier, 1938

### *'Last night I dreamt I went to Manderley again'*

One of the most famous openings in literary history, *Rebecca's* very first line refers to the most described 'character' in the book. Over 428 pages Daphne du Maurier reveals very little about her narrator; we never even learn her given name. Other human players enjoy similarly brief pen portraits. Manderley, however, is described again and again, and by far the most important parts of Maximilian de Winter's sprawling, coastal estate, both to du Maurier and her heroine, lie *outside* the walls of the craggy house in the woods.

First published 1938, *Rebecca*'s brooding storyline is reflected throughout the novel via Manderley's grounds. Within the gardens, which by rights are now her own, the imagined spectre of 'the other woman' clings to the new Mrs de Winter like thick Cornish fog. We are never explicitly told that Manderley is in Cornwall, yet even down to the wildflowers flourishing in the hedgerows and around the beach house, the exotic formal gardens, and especially the ambiguously named Happy Valley, we are never in any doubt as to its setting. The warm ocean currents harnessed by the Gulf Stream embrace the United Kingdom's westernmost extremity, encouraging botanical wonders that might struggle elsewhere. Our narrator notes, for example, that before she came to Manderley, she was most accustomed to the 'basic' mauve rhododendron. Indeed, *R. ponticum* grows virtually anywhere moderately temperate and its tough suckers have invaded much of Europe. Manderley's microclimate

Gardens, once cultured and graceful, have been deserted and given way to botanical anarchy

supports less rugged rhododendron cultivars, such as the unnamed 'blood red' variety that smothers a wall so ominously in our heroine's imagination. The pervasive perfume of azalea that she associates with Rebecca – fresh but overpowering in the woodlands, cut and displayed in vases supplied by the sinister Mrs Danvers, desiccated and nauseating in Rebecca's abandoned wardrobe – also conjures the great historical gardens of Cornwall.

The novel opens with a dream/nightmare of a ruined Manderley, the ancient estate run to chaos. As yet we do not know how it became like this – or even if the image is true. Our narrator is saddened by the house, but its broken grounds truly disturb her, as she passes, phantom-like, through padlocked iron gates, their great spikes rusted with neglect. Gardens, once cultured and graceful, have been deserted and given way to botanical anarchy. Our drab, nameless second Mrs de Winter describes drab, 'nameless shrubs' that have entered into an 'alien marriage' with fifty-foot rhododendrons. She depicts horrors: 'monster shrubs'; a lilac 'mated' with a copper beech; rooks circling the woods; terraced lawns hijacked by Nature 'come into her own again'.

To the modern reader this description might invoke another Cornish vision: the once-Lost Gardens of Heligan, discovered like Sleeping Beauty in the 1990s and restored from dense jungle to perfect health, and there is much to connect the two, if only in location and decay. Manderley *is* based on two real estates, but neither of those is Heligan, which was still very much lost in du Maurier's day. Milton Hall in Cambridgeshire, which

du Maurier visited in 1917, aged 10, inspired the mansion's interiors. These are luxurious but, even in the case of the sinister West Bedroom, might, frankly, be anywhere and in any country house. Manderley's location – in dense woodlands by the sea – and atmosphere – at once both homely and overbearing – can be only one real property: Menabilly.

The ancestral seat of the Rashleigh family since the sixteenth century, Menabilly sits on the Gribben peninsula on Cornwall's south coast. When du Maurier first happened upon the house, on holiday in 1926, it had fallen into disrepair. She would become obsessed with it and eventually, after persuading the then-owner C.S. Rashleigh to lease it to her in 1943, live there. This was, of course, several years after *Rebecca*'s publication; notably she did not live at Menabilly when she wrote the book.

She was instead living in Alexandria, the unwilling 'trailing spouse' to her husband, an officer in the Grenadier Guards. Her father had recently died, her independence was compromised and she was homesick beyond measure for her beloved Cornwall. Miserable, pregnant, resentful, trying to play the compliant 'officer's wife' while wrestling with a fiercely independent nature, it has been suggested that du Maurier's two Mrs de Winters – the rebel and the submissive – represent conflicting sides of her own personality. The second Mrs de Winter's bleak descriptions of a strange, nomadic half-life 'somewhere' else – abroad, but non-specific – carry an autobiographical sense of melancholy. 'We can never go back,' she tells us, though in reality, du Maurier did exactly that. She would spend 24 years restoring Menabilly (and setting another novel, *The King's*

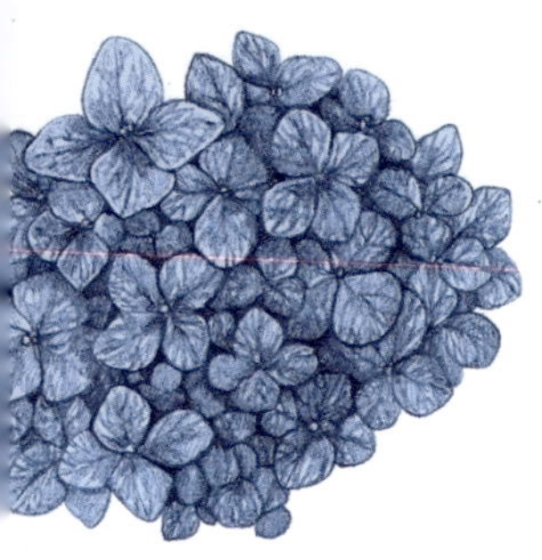

*General*, there) before reluctantly returning the estate to the family in 1969. She could not have known this happier future while writing *Rebecca*, however, and her narrator's claim that imagined foxgloves and pink campions of Manderley's hedgerows can somehow obliterate the 'scrubby vineyards' and 'crumbling stones' of her latest stopping place feel like desperate cries from du Maurier's own soul.

In the searing Egyptian heat, Menabilly danced in her imagination, glimpsed through the dreams of her anonymous heroine. Even there, however, the rain-drenched, wooded garden is haunted: a woman in evening dress, the sound of footsteps, the imprint of a satin shoe in the gravel. Is it the narrator's shoe, or that of some other Cinderella? Later, we learn that her first real glimpse of Manderley was more prosaic: a garishly tinted picture postcard. Perhaps this, too, is autobiographical.

Maximilian de Winter tells his prospective bride nothing about himself, instead using the garden's description like a lure: the daffodils, the crocuses, the sea slate-grey in the background. He talks of the 'vulgar' wildflowers, he won't have them in the house as they would fade there. Only cultivated blooms are brought indoors, he announces, nudging at his young fiancé's powerful sense of insecurity. Even so, she allows herself to fantasize about how, as his wife, they would walk together in Manderley's gardens.

The novel's themes and events are reflected in the estate's grounds. The sloping, terraced lawns, safe, manicured, but providing nowhere to hide from the dark figure watching from the house. The woodlands, whose paths divide, both in choices for the second Mrs de Winter, and in loyalty for Jasper the spaniel, who appears to favour the first incumbent. The reader shares the heroine's profound sense of claustrophobia as Maxim drives through blood-red walls of rhododendron with the cheerful promise of more walls later, this time blue hydrangeas. Instead of the best bedroom with a view over the sea, she is installed in the old visitors' wing, with a view over the least personal area, the rose garden. We do not believe Maxim when he claims it as a place of peace. Even the little beach house in the cove, abandoned since Rebecca's death, is described in terms of its plants: surrounded by stinging nettles.

To her disappointment, Maxim does not personally show his new wife round the garden, delegating the job to his estate manager. When they do finally visit together, he takes her to the most enigmatic part of Manderley. The Happy Valley is a secret garden, away from the cove, with a tinkling stream, birdsong and rhododendrons in pastel shades, that are definitely not blood red. There is, du Maurier tells us, no tangled undergrowth here, no dark trees, yet the heady scent of azalea, so appealing at first, heralds a new darkness even as the petals fall into our heroine's hand.

As the novel progresses, the gardens appear less often, so that when they are mentioned, they hold even more resonance. After the party, Rebecca's little stone satyr, peeping from his verdant clearing, plays his pipes as though in triumph. Later, standing at the West Bedroom window with Mrs Danvers, the second Mrs de Winter cannot tell how far down the tubs of hydrangea are. How much of the fog below is true Cornish mist, and how much is in her mind? The narrator is walking through the garden at the bittersweet moment where she finally begins to realize that Manderley is hers – just a single page before the revelations that lead into the novel's climax.

Du Maurier even uses flowers in the moment where her narrator finally asserts herself, taking scissors to the roses and arranging them in the vases she wants to use. Even so, waiting for the inquest, she restricts herself to the gardens directly next to the house. Manderley's woodlands have become reflections of the weather's heat and oppression.

Our last vision of Manderley by daylight is early morning, wreathed in mist. Its flowers droop with the weight of the previous night's rain, but the birds are awake, and soon the rest of the household will be too. Life will go on, and the second Mrs de Winter dares to dream that all will be well. Yet the reader knows, from the very opening of the novel (which du Maurier originally wrote as a postscript) that this cannot be. Even as she returns, Mrs de Winter closes her eyes, trying to dream of the Happy Valley, but cannot recall it to mind.

# The Enchanted Garden

## 'The Enchanted Garden'
Italo Calvino, 1949

*'There was a long, sombre boom. The two children crouched down behind a clump of ranunculus'*

Hand in hand, Giovannino and Serenella play along the simmering hot railway girders, balancing, skipping, jumping, keeping an eye out for crabs on the sea-side of the track. They will go as far as the tunnel, then turn back, for danger lurks in the cave.

A telegraph wire pings. A train is coming. There is no sign yet of the smoke-belching monster, but the children scramble out of the way up the hillside anyway, preferring the prospect of nettle stings to the spiky grey aloes on the rocky beach.

Giovannino vanishes through a hole in the hedge. A second later, he holds out his hand and helps Serenella through. On all fours in a flower bed, their hair matted with dry leaves and moss, they stare at the magical garden they have stumbled upon.

Italo Calvino is famous for his flights of fantasy, for taking an idea and playing with it. We can see this done structurally, as in *If on a Winter's Night a Traveller*, where the reader is taken through various poorly bound copies of the same novel, or thematically, like *Invisible Cities*, a deceptively simple series of pen portraits depicting 55 fantasy cities that may be read in many ways. Yet Calvino was also the author/editor of the seminal 1956 collection of *Italian Folktales*, and his lifelong love for legend and fairy

## The children are torn. They want to play in this magical place, but they fear being discovered

stories was crucial to his more neo-realist work. The invisible train in 'The Enchanted Garden', for example, might be a mighty, fire-breathing dragon of yore, the garden itself could be the rose grove of *Beauty and the Beast*. As a child Calvino also adored swashbuckling adventures by the likes of Robert Louis Stevenson.

The children creep further through winding paths of eucalyptus into this manicured paradise, encountering only a flight of 'chattering sparrows'. They are uneasy. Trespassers never fare well in fairy stories. Who tends these neat rows of petunias? Who sweeps the leaves from the balustrades, clips the box hedges? In the distance, a smart villa stands in for the traditional 'enchanted castle', its 'flashing windowpanes' a blank as to what lies within.

Calvino loved the romance of gardens from early on. He was born in Cuba in 1923, where his botanist parents were working as tropical agronomists. The family returned to their hometown, Sanremo, on the Italian Riviera when he was still very young. As his father experimented with various vegetables, young Italo was drawn to the maritime forests on the steep cliffsides tumbling into the Mediterranean. He would also have been familiar with the famous railway line that hugs the Riviera coastline, darting in and out of tunnels, one side of the track vertiginous hill, the other craggy, rocky beach.

The children are torn. They want to play in this magical place, but they fear being discovered. They creep along the gravel paths but cannot resist an abandoned, squeak-wheeled wheelbarrow. Giovannino gives

Serenella a ride, keeping the noise down by moving slowly, plucking flowers for her until she has a bouquet. The reader is strongly reminded of *The Secret Garden* (see pages 8–15).

The swimming pool before them is filled to the brim. Again, they are tempted. It is such a hot day, and the water looks so cool. Calvino is very careful to tell us the children are wearing bathing suits. They are not naked. This is not the Garden of Eden. They splash quietly but are not enjoying it as much as they should be.

Beside the pool they see a ping pong table. More temptation. But what if they're discovered? The children play, using light taps until – horrors – Giovannino accidentally sends the ball flying. It strikes a nearby dinner gong, which resounds across the garden.

Hiding behind a clump of ranunculus, the children watch two servants arrive bearing trays of tea, milk and sponge cake, then disappear. Who are they? And where are the gardeners in this place?

The first story in *The Crow Comes Last*, the collection from which 'The Enchanted Garden' is taken, may at least partially answer these questions. In 'Adam, One Afternoon', Libereso, a young anarchist gardener, introduces a servant girl to wildlife via a series of gifts comprising small animals – a snake, a hedgehog, a toad. Yet this boy, so like Dickon in *The Secret Garden* was real. The son of an Esperanto-loving anarchist Libereso ('Liberty' in Esperanto) Guglielmi was the Calvino family's gardener. Wild and exciting, this barefooted nature-boy was the polar opposite of shy, serious, 15-year-old Italo, but the two became friends. Libereso would also appear as Cosimo Piovasco di Rondò, an eighteenth-century nobleman who runs away to a life of adventure in an arboreal kingdom in *The Baron in the Trees*.

Giovannino and Serenella drink the tea and eat the cake but their fear of being discovered trespassing renders the treats tasteless. Eventually, they tiptoe to the villa and peer through a window. Beneath cases of pinned butterflies, a small, pale boy in pyjamas sits on a chaise-longue reading a book. He looks even more anxious than they are. The children's hearts pound. Is the villa enchanted? Is this sick rich boy as trapped as the butterflies? Once again, we are reminded of *The Secret Garden* but now the romance is fading. The pyjama-clad invalid is not Colin Craven. Reality has encroached. For all his wealth the boy cannot enjoy his privileged world any more than the children outside can. The place appears to be under a spell, 'the residue of some injustice committed long ago'.

Clouds cover the sun. In silence, Giovannino and Serenella retrace their steps. They crawl through the hedge, back to the beach and immediately invent a new game throwing seaweed at each other. Calvino implies that neither of them will speak of this again, but he does add one strange detail: 'And Serenella never once cried'.

# Wonderlands

## *Alice's Adventures in Wonderland*
## *Through the Looking-Glass*
## Lewis Carroll, 1865, 1872

*"'We can talk,' said the Tiger Lily, 'when there's anyone worth talking to'"*

Lewis Carroll's seminal fantasy adventures contain some of the most memorable gardens in literature. Today, it is sometimes difficult to remember which garden appears in which novel, thanks to a succession of film and television adaptations fusing elements of both books. Indeed, it is not entirely clear as to whether the two worlds – Wonderland and Looking-Glass Land – are separate entities or aspects of the same fantastical universe. While a re-read will remind us of individual incidents, it is unlikely that particular question will ever be completely answered.

Both tales are episodic, following Alice as she encounters bizarre characters and creatures, but each has a similar objective: she wants to find a beautiful garden that she has glimpsed from afar. *Alice's Adventures in Wonderland* sees her wandering vaguely towards her goal. *Through the Looking-Glass and what Alice Found There*, by contrast, is specifically ordered. As a pawn in gigantic game of chess she must follow the rules of the game.

In *Wonderland*, we first join Alice in a garden, sitting with her sister on a bank, whether a riverbank or simple grassy mound is unclear. Her sister is reading. Alice is bored.

There have been scores of attempts by people to track down the 'real' Wonderland, the places in our world that, turned on their heads, become a nonsense-land for Alice to figure out. Some of these theories are more tenuous than others. Charles Lutwidge Dodgson (Carroll's real name) never visited the Liddell family at their holiday home in Llandudno, for example. Indeed, he told his first 'Alice' story before the property was purchased. This did not stop David Lloyd George unveiling a statue of the white rabbit there in 1933, confidently laying claim to a Welsh Wonderland. A more recent suggestion, by researcher Fiona Davison, that the Queen of Hearts's rose garden was inspired by the work of Henry Bailey, Head Gardener at Nuneham Park in Oxfordshire, visited by Carroll on a boating trip, seems more convincing. Most claims, however, centre around the city of Oxford. One of the largest university colleges, Christ Church, and the Cathedral Deanery, are usually cited as his most likely horticultural muses, but the famous Botanic Garden, founded in 1621, is also mentioned in dispatches.

There is no doubt over Carroll's human muse, ten-year-old Alice Liddell, who he met with her sisters while out photographing the cathedral on 25 April 1856. Daughters of Dean Henry Liddell, they instantly hit it off with the young sub-librarian. Famously, he invented a story for them during a picnic boat trip from Folly Bridge to Port Meadow in 1862. Equally famously, Alice begged him to write it down for her. The handwritten result, *Alice's Adventures Underground* would briefly become *Alice in Elfland* before settling as *Alice's Adventures in Wonderland*, published in 1865 by 'Lewis Carroll' – a complicated play on Latin versions of Dodgson's birthname.

Alice is slowly drifting to sleep when she suddenly notices a white rabbit. He takes a watch from his waistcoat pocket, pronounces himself 'late', and disappears. Alice follows, and falls down one of the world's most famous literary portals, a rabbit hole.

At the bottom she is confronted by many doors, but the tiny golden key she has found fits only one, equally minute. Plausible arguments have been made for the door's inspiration as the one in the wall between the deanery and the cathedral gardens, kept strictly private by a canon who disliked intruders. The Liddell children would not have been allowed through, rendering whatever lay behind it particularly intriguing. Peering through the tiny door, Alice spies the most beautiful garden she has ever seen.

Alice's adventures see her changing size on a regular basis. Courtesy of a bottle marked DRINK ME, she continues her journey.

Several adventures later, as a giant again, she accidentally knocks the poor rabbit into his own cucumber frame. The delightful domesticity of this 'everyday' garden – though even here things are topsy-turvy; the gardener digs for, rather than picks, apples – will contrast with the later formality of the royal grounds.

Having eaten a cake, Alice is tiny again. She must learn to regulate her size. Peeping from behind a blade of grass she spots a caterpillar on a toadstool, smoking a hookah. The Victorians were fascinated by mind-altering drugs but Carroll himself, a non-smoking moderate drinker unimpressed with opium, is unlikely to have sampled the effects of *Amanita muscaria* (fly agaric) as some theories have suggested. Neither his own sketch nor Sir John Tenniel's illustration of the caterpillar's mushroom depicts the famously spotted fungus, but it is possible he had read about the hallucinogenic effects of certain fungi and played on the idea for his own crazy world. Historian Michael Carmichael has pointed out that a few days before Dodgson began writing *Alice in Wonderland,* he made his only visit to the Bodleian Library where Mordecai Cooke's 1860 drug survey *The Seven Sisters of Sleep* had just been deposited. We will never know if the dates are purely coincidental.

Much of *Alice's Adventures in Wonderland* takes place in various woodlands, as Alice searches for her garden. The deanery grounds were largely laid to lawn but did have trees. Some claim the branches of one particularly ancient chestnut resemble those in which the Cheshire Cat appears and disappears, but there is no evidence for this.

We can be sure of Carroll's love for games though, and in the same way he would use chess as a theme in his sequel, he portrays the royal court of Wonderland as a deck of cards. The Queen of Heart's gardeners are, naturally, spades. Alice catches them painting some erroneously planted white roses red; more lethally, so does the queen. They are carted away to the sound of her famous cry 'Off with their heads!'

Before the execution, however, there is time for another game. While essentially ancient, the rules for croquet had only been finalized in the 1850s, and the craze was sweeping England. Dodgson even photographed players, with mallets and balls, rather than, alas, the flamingos and hedgehogs used in Wonderland. Some suggest the famous Tenniel illustration of the game includes, in the background, the roof

## A bed of flowers surprises Alice when she discovers that they can not only talk, but do so quite rudely

of the waterlily house at Oxford Botanic Garden. If this is true, it also involves some artistic licence.

Alice's final act in Wonderland is to destroy the world, which explodes into a shower of cards. As she awakens, they become leaves from the tree under which she has fallen asleep.

Despite some claims to the contrary, *Alice's Adventures in Wonderland* received mainly good reviews on publication. It was a popular success, which encouraged Carroll to write again. This time he exchanged playing-card gardeners for a gigantic horticultural chessboard marked by brooks and neat green hedges. Alice enters Looking-Glass Land via the mirror over the fireplace, so this time, instead of being topsy-turvy, everything is seen in reverse.

Most of the action takes place in the various woodland clearings that make up the board, but once again, Alice's goal is to cross to a garden. First, however, she must meet the flowers in the border of the back-to-front house she is leaving. A bed of flowers with a willow tree growing in the middle surprises her when she discovers that they can not only talk but do so quite rudely. The rose thinks she doesn't look very clever. The daisies chime in – her petals don't curl enough; she looks as though she is wilting. Alice gives as good as she gets, threatening to pick the flowers if they don't hold their tongues. On wondering why they can talk she is told to feel the ground. The soil is caked hard. Most beds are too soft, she learns, and the plants are always asleep.

There is one other flower in the garden that can move like Alice. She is much bushier, and her petals are shorter, worn spikily around the head. She is also red. In *Alice on the Stage*, Carroll described the Red Queen, his Looking-Glass counterpart to the Queen of Hearts, as 'the concentrated essence of all governesses'. She is allegedly based on the Liddell daughters' own governess, the aptly named Miss Prickett.

It is the Red Queen who shows Alice the countryside below, laid out as a chessboard. She sniffs when Alice admires it, claiming '*I've* seen gardens, compared with which this would be a wilderness', but softens a little when Alice asks to join the game, allowing her to stand in for the White Queen's baby daughter. As a pawn she will move two squares in her first move, so Alice takes the train into her new adventure.

For all the theories dreamed up about the real places that inspired Lewis Carroll's fantasy universe, it is worth remembering one thing: this is Wonderland, a land of wonders, where wonders happen. Wonderland may reflect reality, but it isn't real, it cannot exist in our world, and that, surely, is the point.

# The Lost and Perhaps Mythical Labyrinth of Ts'ui Pên

## 'The Garden of Forking Paths'
### Jorge Luis Borges, 1941

*'I leave to various future times, but not to all, my garden of forking paths'*

By 1948 readers of *Ellery Queen's Mystery Magazine* were used to a bi-monthly diet of science fiction and detective stories just that little bit above the ordinary. Championing authors such as Dashiell Hammett, Margery Allingham and Agatha Christie, editor Frederic Dannay's tastes went beyond the general pulp fare found on post-depression newsstands. Even so, it is unlikely readers were entirely ready for Argentinian author Jorge Luis Borges's 'The Garden of Forking Paths', published in translation in August that year, plunging them into what we might now call 'multiverse theory'. Today, thanks to mainstream entertainment franchises, even children can vaguely imagine numerous concurrently existing worlds. In the 1940s alternate histories within quantum mechanics were somewhat less common.

Originally published in Spanish in 1941, the story is short – not 5,000 words – yet it manages to be a puzzle box of many layers. We open with an editorial voice telling us about a British offensive during the First World War postponed, apparently, due to adverse weather conditions. We are then immediately wrongfooted by learning that a deposition made and signed by a Dr Yu Tsun, a captured spy for the German Imperial forces, will shed new light on the decision. Adding further to the mystery, the first two pages of the document are missing.

We join the story as Yu Tsun is about to be uncovered by Captain Richard Madden, somewhere in England. Yu Tsun thinks of his impending death, remembering a garden of his childhood, 'one of the symmetrical gardens of Hai Feng' in Guangdong province, China. He empties his pockets; among the usual detritus he finds a revolver and a single bullet. Is he considering suicide? Even as he ponders 'all things happen to a man precisely, precisely now', a more urgent image pervades his thoughts. Madden's 'long horseface' brings Yu Tsun to his senses and a new decision.

Yu Tsun's movements now revolve around the choices he makes, large and small. We get the feeling that at any point he might have chosen differently, and the story would have ended another way. Things happen by coincidence and accident; his actions are determined by what is available at the time.

As he travels to the village of Ashgrove, he considers his options, remembering some old advice about always turning left, reminding him of similar suggestions he has heard for finding the centre of puzzle mazes. Yu Tsun is, he tells us, the great grandson of Ts'ui Pên, a governor of Yunnan, who gave up everything to spend 13 years labouring over two tasks: an immense novel and a maze 'in which all men would lose themselves'.

Given directions by children who seem to know where he is going, he encounters roads that keep branching, filled with mists and possibilities. Strange music filters in and out of his mind. He meditates on his ancestor's 'lost and perhaps mythical labyrinth' but even that keeps changing its aspect, location and construction in his mind, 'a maze of mazes' that seems to be eternally growing, in both the past and future. Presently he finds himself at a high iron gate, beyond which a tree-lined avenue leads to a pavilion. A man approaches with a lantern and welcomes him to the Garden of Forking Paths.

It would not be productive to ask about Borges's own liking – or not – for horticultural gardens, as his Garden of Forking Paths is neither a real nor an imagined literal garden. Borges is interested in the idea of mazes within the mind. Sometimes described as the link between modernism and post modernism, his is a world of magical realism, constructed and partially deconstructed, based around the choices one makes – or might make.

Inside the house, Yu Tsun meets the mysterious Stephen Albert. He tells Yu Tsun that, for all his ancestor's privations and 13 years of toil, when he died, instead of a novel and a maze, all that was found was 'a shapeless mass of contradictory rough drafts', which, perhaps unwisely, were published by a monk. Yu Tsun is shown a lacquered cabinet containing the result and finally understands that it contains both book and labyrinth, for the book *is* the labyrinth. 'The Garden of Forking Paths,' Albert tells him, is 'an enormous riddle, or parable, whose theme is time'.

It would be too simplistic to imagine Borges's story in the same way as the 1970s children's book series *Choose Your Own Adventure*... where at the end of each section, the reader decides what should happen next and, depending on their choices, the story results in a different narrative every time, not least in that the reader does not get to choose any of the outcomes. Even the modern genre of hypertext fiction, where the reader chooses links that will take them down an almost infinite number of alternative routes, seems a facile comparison. In many ways, however, that is exactly what Borges seems to be suggesting 'The Garden of Forking Paths' is the result of. Stephen Albert tells Yu Tsun that his ancestor did not consider time as linear, but a series of infinite times that diversify into a web that covers every possibility, in which we may or may not exist.

Borges was interested in the work of many philosophers, including George Bishop Berkeley, who developed a theory of 'immaterialism' – that nothing really exists and can only be brought into being when perceived by the viewer – and Arthur Schopenhauer, who suggested that the ultimate nature of everything is will. The route Yu Tsun takes may just as easily have been any number of alternatives.

Slowly understanding, the cornered spy senses the dew-damp garden outside is 'infinitely saturated' with invisible people. Only one figure is clear to him: Richard Madden.

Yu Tsun makes his final choice.

# Imaginary Species

'When the sukebind is in bud...'

*Cold Comfort Farm*, Stella Gibbons, 1932

A frequent gripe by pedantic crime fiction readers is that the deadly qualities from one or other plant couldn't possibly have inflicted the injuries described by the author. Plants are, indeed, extraordinary but they cannot always perform to order when the creative juices are in full flow. Why not, then, just invent a new plant that does everything the plot needs?

The most pernickety of all murder weapons, fungi enjoy their own natural kingdom today, but they were still treated alongside plants in 1923, when Ernest Bramah's blind detective Max Carrados investigated *The Mystery of the Poisoned Dish of Mushrooms*. Carrados discovers that the deadly active ingredient that kills Charlie Winpole within half an hour of his ingesting the dish is bhurine. Like *Amanita bhuroides*, the mushroom species bhurine is found in, however, it does not exist. Neither does the deadly *Purple pileus* of H.G. Wells's eponymous 1896 story of suicidal tendencies.

Fictional plants are not always murderous. Stella Gibbon's sukebind in *Cold Comfort Farm* (1932) seems to represent nothing less than human lust. Its pungent scent comes 'swooning' to meet the night air; its long, pink buds and large flowers burst like 'snarling fangs', showing the shameless heart that sends out 'full gusts of sweetness'. Like all such dangerous things, however, sukebind also represents darkness. It cannot be allowed to romp uncurbed and is slowly eradicated.

Authors who create their own detailed worlds often populate them with created plant life too. J.R.R. Tolkien's Middle Earth enjoys dozens of invented plants including several strains of pipe weed, among them Southern Star, Longbottom Leaf and Gandalf's favourite, Old Toby.

## Its pungent scent comes 'swooning' to meet the night air, its long, pink buds and large flowers burst like 'snarling fangs'

Athelas (aka kingsfoil, aka 'a weed') is one of the few things that will temporarily treat a wound inflicted by a Morgul blade, while the Ents are an entire race of tree-like forest herders. J.K. Rowling's fantasy world in the *Harry Potter* books has even more invented plants, good and evil. The Whomping Willow in Hogwart's grounds is one of an important but highly aggressive species, to be treated with the same caution as devil's snare, which will strangle anything in its path, while mandrakes, an augmented version of the real *Mandragora officinarum*, weave ancient folklore with modern invention. Mandrake is a useful herb, as is gillyweed, a seaweed-like plant that allows the consumer to breath underwater.

The author as the god of their own invented universe both gives and takes away when it comes to plants.

# The Garden

## *Tom's Midnight Garden*
Philippa Pearce, 1958

*'There is a time between night and day when landscapes sleep'*

Children's literature provides a rich seam of 'secret gardens', worlds that only young people and, occasionally, one or two trusted grown-ups can locate. Usually, the barrier between such gardens and the adult world is a wall or hedge, providing a small frisson of danger that the secret may be discovered at any time. In *Tom's Midnight Garden* the boundary is far less easy to breach: it is Time itself. The peril here is primeval. At any moment Tom may either be unable to cross into the past or, worse, become stuck there with no passage back to his present.

In the first few pages, the reader is fooled into thinking *Tom's Midnight Garden* is another *Secret Garden*-esque, 'angry child tamed' story (see pages 8–15), as Tom learns he is to be sent away to stay with relatives in a big house. However, while initially unsympathetic, he begins to be more likeable more quickly than Mary Lennox. Perhaps this is because we can understand more easily why he is grumpy: he must leave loving parents, a brother and a perfectly enjoyable garden, described in the novel's second paragraph. Small, with a vegetable plot, flower beds, a rough area and an apple tree, it is nothing to the splendour he will later discover, but is nevertheless a small paradise to two brothers planning a tree house.

The unnamed mansion he is sent to is large and rambling but, unlike *The Secret Garden's* Misselthwaite Manor, has been divided into apartments.

Broad brushstrokes tell of a great lawn, with flower beds, a 'beetle-browed yew' and a glasshouse the size of a real house

It has not even been converted sympathetically. Aunt Gwen and Uncle Alan live in a tiny part and one of Tom's bedroom windows is barred like a nursery. The bathroom window has similar 'prison' bars; we later discover the two were once part of a single room. Worse, there is no garden, just a mean backyard full of dustbins.

Philippa Pearce had good reason to describe the house this way, as she is talking about her own childhood home. Born in Great Shelford, Cambridgeshire, Pearce grew up in the Mill House, playing in the same garden her miller father had played in, and her grandfather before that. In an agrarian world milling was a prosperous profession, but the postwar industrialization of commodities like flour meant the family had to sell up. Despite its bucolic meadow setting by the river Cam and surrounded by a beautiful walled garden, the house was no longer attractive to people moving towards the cities and seemed in grave danger of demolition. Pearce imagined what would happen if her childhood sanctuary was turned into flats, a claustrophobic prison of tiny cells instead of the idyllic playground she had once known.

The one constant is the ancient grandfather clock in the shared hallway, which has lived so long in the house it is rusted into the very walls. We quickly learn two things: that it keeps strange hours and its chimes can be heard throughout the house. When the clock strikes 13, Tom is intrigued enough to get out of bed and explore.

The midnight garden is, like the house, directly inspired by Pearce's memories of her own garden. Broad brushstrokes tell of a great lawn, with flower beds, a 'beetle-browed yew' and a glasshouse the size of a real house. The description is not complete, however. Like all the best gardens, we are teased by paths that twist away, walls and hedges that whisper of delights around the corner. Like Tom, we are desperate to explore further.

Pearce gently eases us into the idea of time travel by showing us a different hallway when Tom returns, with people who cannot see him and disappear like ghosts. There is much play with the idea of ghosts throughout the book; it is never clear just who is haunting whom, and while death is rarely mentioned, Pearce includes small hints along the way, for example the asparagus beds, with their 'grave-like mounds'.

On his return to the 1950s, Tom's overwhelming emotion, however, is one of happiness. Indeed, almost every time he visits the garden it is summer, albeit at different times of the day, and filled with good cheer. He explores a couple more times to establish the 'rules' by which this strange world exists, but although he can feel himself watched he is not yet aware of who tends the garden. We learn that he is no gardener himself, but he is a tree-climber, lending us a new perspective: from the air. He tries to push his way through a door, succeeding only in a limited and most uncomfortable way. Stubbornly part-corporeal, he is no ghost, but neither can he touch or be seen by anyone – or at least that's what he believes.

Adults, as is so common in children's books, do not understand Tom's experiences. His aunt and uncle are, respectively, indulgent and snide, he instead confides in his brother Peter, ill in bed at home, marking his letters 'private' and 'confidential' and instructing Peter to burn after reading. By now Tom is fully committed to exploration, but Pearce ups the ante by giving us a deadline: he is to return home in ten days' time. This becomes a problem when, just a few lines later, he encounters someone in the garden who can see him.

Hatty is, she informs him, a princess. Carrying a stick and a half-eaten apple, against a background of yew, she does seem to reign over this garden kingdom, though Tom is never in any doubt that she is just a child like himself. He is, however, surprised to learn she has been watching him for a long time. As she shows her new friend around the garden, Hatty names the plants there, again reminding us that this is a real place. Tom shudders at the sight of a castor oil plant and tortures the leaves of a sensitive plant. He always means to ask his aunt and uncle about the garden, but never remembers when he wakes up. Like Pearce herself as a child, he lives in the dreamlike moment. On one visit, a storm fells a tree, the next it is unharmed; time here is not always linear. He is, however, largely unaware of time changes within the garden, save when he is taken back to a vision of Hatty as a very small child who is taken in as charity case after the death of her parents. Even when she complains that he is leaving it longer and longer between visits, he replies only that he comes every night, and does not think about the implications of her words.

Tom is only too aware of time running out in his own period, however. He is disappointed to discover that the old lady living upstairs moved in only recently, as he had hoped to ask her about the house's history. Now he must discover it for himself. He engineers a little more time, feeling the guilt of leaving his brother alone in quarantine with only letters for company, while he continues his nocturnal visits to the garden.

There is one other character that we follow in the past, though unlike Ben Weatherstaff in *The Secret Garden*, the deeply religious Abel is not a friend. The moment when he turns around and Tom realizes that he is looking directly at him is chilling. 'Get you back to hell, where you came from!' he commands. To Abel, Tom is no ghost; he is the devil himself come to tempt Hatty into ruin.

As the story moves inside the house, Tom becomes out of his depth. We readers are equally lost. Time is marching on and only the garden is safe, only the garden remains the same. Hatty says as much when they finally meet again, when she tells him he is 'thinner' – not in weight but in substance. She entices him out of the garden, telling him it will always be there but the great frost that has frozen the river is temporary; they must take advantage of it now.

Tom is out of time, in more ways than one but it takes his brother to point out what he has – perhaps wilfully – never noticed before. Peter dreams himself into Tom's world and is horrified to find Tom's 'little girl' friend is a grown woman. Shaken at his brother's words, and Hatty's subsequent behaviour on his return to the garden, Tom discovers his way back to the future is blocked. His horrors result in a time-travelling scream, waking the entire modern-day house – and the inhabitant of the top floor.

# Time is marching on and only the garden is safe, only the garden remains the same

One of the many great joys of Philippa Pearce's work is that nothing is wasted. Everything mentioned earlier in *Tom's Midnight Garden* will have some part to play later, making for satisfying – and multiple – re-reads. The clues as to why all this is happening are sprinkled like breadcrumbs throughout the novel, but only at the end do we understand how they dovetail into the collision of two young lives, decades apart from each other. The common denominator is, of course, the garden Philippa Pearce was so keen to save.

She succeeded, though not for herself. For the last 33 years of her life, she lived in the same village she grew up in, a keen gardener to the end, but in a cottage, with neat rows of vegetables and herbs, near the meadows and river she loved so much. Mill House was neither demolished nor converted. When it went on the market in 2014, the asking price was £3.5 million.

# The Manor Garden

## *Elizabeth and her German Garden*
Elizabeth von Arnim, 1898

### *'May 7th – I love my garden'*

In 1898, Macmillan & Co, London, published an anonymous, apparently autobiographical satire on the mores of late Victorian society and its vogue for books about individuals' gardening successes. The novel (for it was, despite all appearances, fiction) became such a runaway success that by May 1899 it had enjoyed 21 reprintings. Tongues wagged – who could this ebullient, joyous 'Elizabeth' be? Where exactly was the fabulous garden she had apparently revived from wilderness? And who was the mysterious 'Man of Wrath' depicted with equal amounts of deference and dry humour?

*Elizabeth and her German Garden* is still much loved. It is a gardener's garden book, filled with the joy and minutiae that fills a horticulturist's heart. Yet the work's delight in growing things sometimes overshadows other themes, some of which seem darker today than they may have done even at the time.

In time the author, who tried her best to remain anonymous, would be revealed as Australian-born Mary Annette Beauchamp, cousin of New Zealand author Katherine Beauchamp (see 'The Garden Party' by Katherine Mansfield, pages 96–99) and wife of German Count Henning August von Arnim-Schlagenthin. Concerned her husband would not approve of her writing 'commercial fiction', all Beauchamp's books were published as 'by the author of *Elizabeth and her German Garden*'.

# It is a gardener's garden book, filled with the joy and minutiae that fills a horticulturist's heart

The work appeared to be autobiographical, so its 'author' was assumed to be 'Elizabeth'. Eventually Mary Annette became Elizabeth in real life too.

The book is a love letter to gardening. Its very first line 'May 7th – I love my garden' sets the tone for a work steeped in flowers and the recovery of a neglected manor garden somewhere in Germany. No one has lived there for 25 years, rendering it 'less of a garden than a wilderness' but it instantly captures Elizabeth's heart. She delights in its wild plants and the views across meadows, cornfields, sandy heaths and dark forests. Of the grey stone house, we are told little, save that she spends 'reluctant nights' there. She cannot believe they have had this garden for years and chosen to live in the city and even gone to – horrors – the seaside for holidays.

By May 10th she is truly getting stuck into the planting. We learn of the only part of the garden that has been given any care – a privet-edged semicircle, with 11 beds of different sizes around a moss-covered sundial – which she has entirely sown with *Ipomoea*, because she has read that it is 'the only thing needful to turn the most hideous desert into a paradise' and dutifully purchased ten pounds of seed. Paradise does not appear, but she has some sunflowers, sweet peas and hollyhocks ('in rather ugly colours') to punctuate the straggling Madonna lilies. Undeterred, she lists the garden's many varieties of rose, all, bar two, dwarf; there are only two standards in the entire property. Marie van Houtte. Duke of Teck. Cheshunt Scarlet. Prefet de Limburg. Souvenir de la Malmaison… the list is long and intense.

We soon learn that the rest of the neighbourhood thinks her eccentric for spending so much time outdoors. She is serene. Her 'other half' is indulgent of her whims, she tells them, allowing her to spend six weeks alone, ostensibly 'overseeing workmen' in the house. In reality she luxuriates in what used to be a lawn, now a meadow, 'filled with every kind of pretty weed'. She takes a dinner gong to bed to scare away any prurient phantoms and dreams of the nuns that lived here when it was a convent, wondering what they would make of Cell 14 being turned into a bathroom.

Vicariously, we live with Elizabeth's triumphs and mistakes. We rejoice at the majestic 'Jackmanii' clematis, commiserate as the giant poppies droop after being moved. We mourn in July when the rockets* have finished and the delphiniums sag, but rally later in the year as the garden enjoys a renaissance. Each rose is assessed for its beauty and resilience. 'The Viscountess Folkestones and Laurette Messimys have been the most beautiful,' she tells us, 'each flower an exquisite loose cluster of coral-pink petals paling at the base to a yellow-white'. Elizabeth does not even resent (too much) dirtying her clothes 'kneeling before such perfect beauty'.

Like Elizabeth, the von Arnims had moved to Nassenheide in Pomerania (now Rzędziny, Poland). With such detail in the writing – varieties, planting schemes, initial hiccups – it would be easy to assume she is writing directly about Nassenheide itself. This is not necessarily true. E.M. Forster, employed as a tutor to von Arnim's children a few years later, claimed in a 1959 article for *The Listener* that there was not much of a garden at Nassenheide, it was mainly surrounded by paddocks and shrubberies, though there were some flowers, mainly pansies, tulips, roses, and 'endless lupins'.

Elizabeth's garden may be a figment of von Arnim's imagination but that does not make it any less 'true' and what makes it so believable is the 'honesty' with which Elizabeth admits her mistakes. An avid reader of gardening manuals, she does not always have the prior technical knowledge their authors assume.

There has never been a gardener who has not made mistakes, and it would have been refreshing to read about horticultural blunders in a culture where authors boasted only of successes. For all her bucolic delight however, all is not perfect in Elizabeth's garden. As an aristocratic woman,

# There has never been a gardener who has not made mistakes, and it would have been refreshing to read about horticultural blunders in a culture where authors boasted only of successes

she may not do any physical work. Worse, a succession of male gardeners do not want to take orders from a woman either. One gives her notice on the first day of every month, a habit which she takes cheerfully, and is probably the best way to deal with it, but 'if only I could dig and plant myself' she sighs. She once attempted to 'slink out' with a spade and rake during the servants' dinner hour, but it involved too much subterfuge to be repeated.

It would be too simple to call von Arnim a 'feminist' author; there are many conflicting thoughts in her writing, but the burgeoning sense of outrage at the traditional role of women is an often-overlooked theme in *Elizabeth and her German Garden*. 'If Eve had had a spade in Paradise,' she claims, 'we should not have had all that sad business with the apple'.

Elizabeth is out of her depth when she tries to fit in with the local gentry by attending church and dinner parties. She is puzzled when they believe her abandoned, even after she tells them her husband is indulgent of her gardening pleasures. Deciding that 'cooks are the safest subject for conversation', she tries her best but soon realizes that 'I don't know a single person within twenty miles who really cares for his garden or has discovered the treasures of happiness that are buried in it'. The incident depresses her. She is further dejected when she discovers the gardener has planted 'rockets' at the front, masking everything else. Another lesson learned.

The book's episodic style lulls the reader into feeling that von Arnim is writing just for them, filled with confidences and confessions.

Only occasionally does she tip the balance into all-out satire, such as when her gardener has to be sent to an asylum, having taken to going about with a spade in one hand and a revolver in the other. He is replaced by a Russian, lame and with a 'hideous' eye disease, who Elizabeth is shocked to find has a wife and children. She has a little sympathy for her Russian and Polish labourers but reveals a more 'Victorian' view of the world when she says they 'herd together like animals and do the work of animals'. She feels a little more for the women, regularly beaten by their husbands (the Man of Wrath describing it as 'marital muscle') and forced to return to work the instant after giving birth, but her comment that they receive less pay, 'not because they work less but because they are women and must not be encouraged' does not carry enough of a ring of irony for modern-day comfort.

Winter is a time to dream, to make lists for spring and, endearingly, for Elizabeth to become mildly depressed when reflecting upon the probable differences between her ideas and their realization. The new gardener is in love with the cook, not Elizabeth's plans. 'I wish with all my heart I were a man,' she keens.

She is 'inflicted with houseguests', including an annoying young woman author with a bicycle and 'modern' ideas. Unlike her creator, Minora has no sense of irony, failing to see she is being teased when the rest of the party suggest comic titles for her books.

The tedious, indoor winter months are used to further explore the idea of women's rights. Miss Jones the governess makes a stirring speech then leaves; it is unclear whether it is of her own volition. The Man of Wrath – usually a silent background presence – waxes about the shortcomings of Woman, claiming 'she is the victim of her own vanity'. 'Only the strong-minded want to be equals,' he announces, suggesting that the strong-minded are invariably plain. He does admit, however, that 'as soon as they are fit to occupy a better [position] no power on earth will be able to keep them out of it'. Arnim spends 16 pages voicing the Man of Wrath's opinions on women and, being just shy of enough irony to be conclusively satirical, it is not entirely clear what she means by doing so.

By January we are on safer ground once more as Elizabeth plans the coming months in the garden. February has been a frenzy of seed sowing, hotbeds and a discovery: of the joys of manure. Vegetable marrows and primroses are on their way from England.

There may not have been much of a garden at Nassenheide, and the real Elizabeth's Man of Wrath may have been a philanderer from whom she was eventually separated. Her second marriage may not have been idyllic either, but there is no doubting one thing: her love of gardens. In 1930 von Arnim created a rose garden at Mougins in the south of France. She would only be separated from it in 1939, with the looming threat of war.

Katherine Mansfield once pointed out that 'Cousin Elizabeth' had a genuine 'love of flowers' and they burst from every line of *Elizabeth and her German Garden*.

The fictional Elizabeth's last diary entry is for April 18th. Her unwanted guests, dark spectres of discord and winter, are gone. Spring is here. 'Oh, I could dance and sing,' she trills, alone at last, among 'the happy flowers I so much love'.

*Von Arnim mentions 'rockets' many times in the novel. They are probably the sweet or dame's rocket *Hesperis matronalis*, which come in the mauve and white she mentions.

# Mrs Bulpit's Yard

## *The Hanging Garden*
Patrick White, 2012

*'Tree trunks and the branches of trees had knotted like the muscles in men's bodies'*

It is 1942. Eirene Sklavos's mamma is in the next room, telling a marzipan-skinned woman who smells of liquor that her daughter is a quiet, reasonable child. Eirene is not so sure. She looks out of the closed window through the leaves of 'dark yet glossy trees' growing out of a wall across a private-looking bay. She fantasizes that if she were to lift the curtain, she might see the volcano on the next island from her faraway home. She does not yet grasp that she is to be left with the marzipan woman while her mother returns to Greece with a lover. Eirene knows her father died in a prison cell and that the marzipan lady is a stranger. She knows that even though Mamma's sister Aunt Alison lives nearby she is not taking her in. She knows she is not allowed to wave Mamma goodbye. She knows little else, not even – yet – that in this place she will be a 'reffo'.

The other young refugee in Essie Bulpit's benign but alcohol-addled care knows little more. Gilbert Horsfall has been bombed out of his home in England. His mother was killed, but he is more disturbed by the loss of his best friend Nigel, who perished in the same raid. Traipsed across America to an uncertain new life in Australia, bullied at school and neglected in his foster home, he has made himself a life in the hanging garden, and no new kid is getting their hands on it.

Published posthumously, apparently against the author's wishes, *The Hanging Garden* was not an easy choice for inclusion in this book. In his personal biography for *Les Prix Nobel* (he won the Nobel Prize for Literature in 1973) Patrick White revelled in a review that named him 'Australia's most unreadable novelist'. This can be taken many ways, not least in the experimental, postmodernist style(s) he often adopts, but this particular novel was literally unreadable for many years. White began writing *The Hanging Garden* in 1981 as the first part of a trilogy. Friends noted he was pleased with it, but he was constantly interrupted by other projects. At the time of his death in 1990, the book remained incomplete. His will stated that any manuscripts left unfinished should be burnt.

Gil does not want a new 'playmate', especially not a Greek, especially not a girl. The little figlets in the wild garden are his to crush, the earthy smells are his to sniff, the broken statue he found in the fern bank is his to deface. Furious, he hides among the ivy and the creeper until he itches and sneezes. Eirene is equally adamant. 'All the house, the garden must belong to one or other of them. There was nothing they could possibly share'.

As the narrative veers between points of view and toys with first, third and, on occasion, second person perspectives (sometimes changing point of view several times within the same paragraph) the reader quails, trying to work out who is thinking what at any one moment. Eirene? Gilbert? Both? Or one of the disturbingly distant adults that filter in and out of their lives, of whom none are interested in caring for the children.

Forced together and teetering on the edge of puberty, the two finally find solace in the garden that 'hangs' over Neutral Bay. We are not told that White chose this (real) Sydney suburb because during colonial times the city's harbours were zoned – all 'foreign vessels' docked in Neutral Bay – but it is hard not to imagine it was a factor in his decision.

Despite their initial suspicions, the two 'reffos' begin to bond. The garden becomes a haven as they navigate their way through a disjointed life, tolerated but unwanted by the adults around them, providing moments of both innocence and experience. She gets her first period; he grows hair under his arms. Even Mrs Bulpit vaguely notices the junction their lives are approaching. On answering her question about what they are doing up a tree – building a 'cubby' (treehouse) – she sighs 'one minute you're grown up, the next you're kids again'.

The relationship is intense, but it is hard to work out what the exact nature of it is. Even as The Three Events that will change the children's lives forever unfold it is not clear where White is heading. We are left with aching, simple prose that both delights and frustrates. In certain 'heavy' light the hanging garden's paths 'look substantial where the concrete had not crumbled', tree trunks and branches are 'knotted like the muscles in men's bodies'. Rust glowers 'like blood in the act of drying'. After Event Number Three, when Eirene has finally gone to live with her aunt Alison, we are told that the Lockhart garden is a mess, 'full of Ally's failures and Harold's avoidances', yet when Eirene asks if she can return to the hanging garden, her aunt sniffs '*garden* – I'd call it a wilderness'.

Aunt Alison may be right, but we cannot know for certain, because White has veiled the children's paradise to the outside world, including his readers. We can only create a fractured image of the hanging garden, a place that rejects 'even the midday light'. We are given vague impressions of deep shade and steaming heat. If there was a large enough gap in the 'patent leather foliage' we might have a better view of the harbour below, but even when specific plants are mentioned – a mildewed Moreton Bay fig, hibiscus trumpets in the 'lower garden' – we still have no idea what the place *looks like*. The message is clear: we are trespassing. We have no business trying to conjure a cohesive image from such horticultural table scraps. Even the concrete paths that may once have allowed strangers to tread there are now crumbled – any illusion of their solidity is a trick of the noonday light. Mrs Bulpit has long since given up trying.

We cannot know what Patrick White intended for his heroes as he never started books two or three. Arguably, we should not have *The Hanging Garden* at all. Despite his instructions to burn his papers, White's old friend and literary agent Barbara Mobbs claimed that he had shown her the manuscript for *The Hanging Garden*, but not the matches, implying that he had not instructed her to burn it. She also noted that he had personally destroyed anything he had genuinely disliked.

Mobbs sold 32 boxes of White's papers to the National Library of Australia on behalf of the named charities in his will. In 2012, *The Hanging Garden* was transcribed from a handwritten manuscript and published unedited, to international acclaim. It is seen as one of the great Australian novels and considered one of White's finest achievements.

# The Apple Orchard of Cair Paravel

## *The Chronicles of Narnia*
C.S. Lewis, 1950–1956

*'"Have none of you guessed where we are?" said Peter'*

Of all the evocative line drawings made by Pauline Baynes for C.S. Lewis's mid-twentieth century fantasy cycle *The Chronicles of Narnia*, none is more haunting than four post-war schoolchildren staring at the ruins of an ancient castle. Standing in the shadow of a grizzled apple tree, watched by a crumbling stone faun and a strange, exotic bird, they do not yet realize these moss- and ivy-covered walls are the ruins of Cair Paravel, the palace from which they themselves ruled when they were the kings and queens of the land of Narnia.

Last year.

Time moves strangely in Narnia; it is hard to know whether a year or a millennium in human terms has passed. Lewis places 'anchors' in his books: people, places or events that allow us to work out how much time has passed and for us to retain our sense of geography within his realm. Cair Paravel is one of those anchors, appearing in six of the sequence's seven volumes (the castle is not yet constructed in the sixth book, Narnia's origin story, *The Magician's Nephew*). A grand seat of government, the palace is variously peaceful, powerful, abandoned, besieged and overrun. If it does not take part in the action – for example in *The Voyage of the Dawn Treader* – it is a haven of comfort, representing the home the travellers yearn for. Its name is derived from two old English words:

Cair Paravel is a haven of comfort, representing the home the travellers yearn for

*caer* or 'court', and *paravail* meaning 'lesser', reminding us that however grand this court may be, it can only ever exist in the shadow of the great lion Aslan's majesty.

The castle is at its most powerful during Narnia's Golden Age, at the end of the first book, *The Lion, the Witch and the Wardrobe*, after the four Pevensie children have fulfilled the ancient prediction:

*When Adam's flesh and Adam's bone*
*Sits at Cair Paravel in throne*
*The evil time will be over and done*

We do not see very much of it, however. For Lewis, the story finished after the breaking of the great stone table; the rest is mere decoration and set-up for the next book. There is a reason for this: the entire sequence is a Christian allegory, to be interpreted like a journey, along the lines of great theological works such as Bunyan's *The Pilgrim's Progress*.

The orchard at Cair Paravel, full of apples, is not the Garden of Eden. Aslan makes it quite clear that 'his' land is far away from Narnia, but the castle *is* a haven of goodness, and while it prospers so will the land. Again, Pauline Baynes's illustrations help to fill the gaps, majestic visions of a pre-Disney fairytale castle set high on an ocean-washed peninsula, its turrets and great halls circled by seabirds. It has been suggested that Lewis based the palace on the equally romantic Dunluce Castle in Northern Ireland.

At Cair Paravel's height there does not seem to be room for a garden. As kings and queens, the children act regally, even speaking like medieval royalty, but they yearn for nature, for the forest, and for that they must venture beyond the castle walls. It is while thundering through the woods there, hunting the elusive white stag, that they are drawn back into their own world.

As a scholar, Lewis was influenced by the classics – Ovid, Dante, Milton – but as a human he was motivated by humbler sources. As a child he had been unmoved by gardens, but he later spoke with great emotion of a toy 'forest' his brother made from a biscuit tin lid when he was very tiny. A moss 'forest floor', decorated with twigs and flowers, it was 'the first beauty I ever knew'. It gave him a love of nature, and he admitted 'as long as I live my imagination of Paradise will retain something of my brother's toy garden'.

Gardens pop up throughout the Chronicles, from the ironically short-lived Garden of Youth in *The Magician's Nephew*, through the Island of Voices and Ramandu's Island in *The Voyage of the Dawn Treader* to the eternal garden at the end of *The Last Battle*. They are all of them more magical than any garden set in the human world, especially the ghastly shrubbery in the grounds of the ghastlier Experiment House in *The Silver Chair*. They are none of them more evocative than the overgrown apple orchard at Cair Paravel.

Along with the more formal gardens at The Kilns – Lewis's Oxford home, bought in 1930 and where he lived until his death in 1963 – rolled eight acres of woodland and a lake surrounded by trees planted by the author and his brother. Lewis could see the woods from his study window; perhaps on snowy days he imagined a lamp atop a post glowing in the distance. He would write all seven Chronicles from that study and, perhaps unsurprisingly, the landscape was not his only influence. It is rumoured, for example, that the marsh-wiggle Puddleglum in *The Silver Chair* was based on his gardener, and it is difficult not to imagine Lewis himself as the kindly old professor in *The Lion, the Witch and the Wardrobe* when one discovers he took in young evacuees during the Second World War.

By the opening of the second volume, *Prince Caspian*, the last tongue of land linking Narnia's citadel with the mainland has washed away.

Cair Paravel is now an island. When they are whisked away from their railway platform, the children, standing on daisy-studded grass among the ruins, cannot initially work out where they are. They are particularly confused by the great apple orchard giving them such strange sensations.

Even when Peter, formerly High King Peter, begins to realize that 1,300 years have passed in the single human year they have been away, even when he reminds his siblings of the day before they left Narnia, when they themselves planted the orchard, they cannot quite believe it. Memories of the planting itself are strong. Pomona, greatest of the wood people, had cast good spells on the enterprise. Old Lilygloves, chief of the moles – 'decent little chaps' – who'd dug the holes, had told the kings and queens they would be glad of the apples one day. Lucy begins to believe, but Edmund, always the sceptic, points out that the orchard is growing right up to the north gate. 'We wouldn't have been such fools,' he protests, allowing Lewis to explain to new readers how Narnian time works.

Once again, very little 'onstage time' is spent at Cair Paravel; the action swiftly moves elsewhere. It is not even mentioned at the end of the book, and we are left to discover that Caspian rebuilt the castle in the intervening years between his ascension to the Narnian throne and the beginning of *The Silver Chair* when Eustace Scrubb and Jill Pole are blown there by Aslan. Cair Paravel's power – and that of its magical garden – is, instead, 'felt' as a constant throughout the *Chronicles*. *The Horse and His Boy*, which takes place during the Golden Age, portrays the castle as a rallying point for true Narnians, but its power is already teetering as High King Peter has left to vanquish giants. Queen Susan appears to be growing away from the world, only Queen Lucy remains. As Lewis points out in his non-Narnian work, *Four Loves*, a garden 'will not fence or weed itself… it will remain a garden only if someone does all these things to it'. He is speaking, of course, about faith, but he might be talking of Cair Paravel too.

By *The Last Battle*, Cair Paravel's majesty has been compromised. Tirian, last king of Narnia, craves to get away from the bloated pomp of state, but even as Narnia crumbles, we are reminded of the castle's former importance. The four great monarchs are mentioned like talismans: 'they have always come when things were at their worst'.

Near the story's nadir, Farsight the Eagle reports Cair Paravel taken, filled with dead Narnians and living Calormenes. Both characters and the reader believe the king when he announces upon hearing this that Narnia is no more.

Yet this is a story of redemption. Peter, Edmund and Lucy (Susan has grown up and no longer believes in Narnia, a warning to us all), and other favourite characters from earlier novels arrive to save Lewis's invented world. The humans are surprised; they have been told they can never return, yet here they are. They are filled with memories, even Tirian remembers playing in Cair Paravel's gardens, but the end is near. The whole series has been a work of allegory, and we are reaching our own metaphorical deaths. The characters have vanquished the false Aslan and they are rewarded by meeting long-departed friends from previous books, but not even the real Aslan can save the now-corrupted Narnia. Father Time collapses the world, High King Peter closes the door and Aslan leads his faithful to a new place.

A bright procession leads to mountains covered with forests and waterfalls and orchards, even sweeter than the one at Cair Paravel. The path narrows as the human England draws nearer and Lucy fears they will once more be sent back to Earth. Yet this is the Last Battle. In something of a surprise move, Aslan reveals that in the real world there has been a train accident in which the human children died. At last they may stay here, with him, because it is only the beginning of the Great Story, 'which goes on forever'.

# The Court Gardens of the Empress of Japan

## *The Pillow Book*
## Sei Shōnagon, *c.*1000

*'Wisteria flowers. Snow on plum blossoms'*

Sometimes a book is so seminal it gives birth to a genre of its own. Sei Shōnagon's tenth century miscellany of gossip, anecdotes, opinions and general whimsy is one such work, inspiring the Japanese literary form *zuihitsu*, which comprises unrelated reflections and personal literary fragments into a single text. In the Western world such works might be classified as 'commonplace books' but few, even in Japan, will be as personal as the most famous (though perhaps not the very first) example. Shōnagon's *Pillow Book* – perhaps made from paper that might stuff a pillow or something to be kept under one's pillow, the exact explanation is unclear – discusses opinions, incidents, lovers, intrigues and curiosities, naming names alongside lists of correct behaviour, etiquette and dress codes at the Heian court. Shōnagon also makes lists – many of them – of things that delight, shock, entertain or disgust her. Her work is the largest single source of information about court life in tenth-century Japan, but it is also recognizably human. Shōnagon has the same passions, interests and emotions as us. She suffers the same indignities and inflicts the same occasional cruelties that we might. Her life is conducted in the private mansions and semi-public areas of the palace; her (many) romantic trysts take place on verandas, behind slatted screens and in the various gardens of her mistress, the Empress Fujiwara no Teishi, First Consort of the Emperor Ichijō, often under cover of darkness.

Life revolved around the Empress, and the action of *The Pillow Book* takes place almost exclusively in her court, both indoors and out. Like so many other such environments, it is a world of jealousies and intrigues, and Shōnagon is just as susceptible as any other. Her frankness does not always show her in the best light, but she clearly adores her mistress, a benign presence who loves her garden, however difficult her life would later become.

The Heian period saw the zenith of high s shinden style, including courtyard gardens with small streams, ponds, islands, pavilions and bridges, both arched and flat. An open space in front of the main hall of a palace or mansion might also include a gravel-covered area for entertainments and rituals. A good description of such a garden may be found in *The Tale of Genji* by Murasaki Shikibu. Murasaki was lady-in-waiting to the Emperor Ichijō's Second Consort, Empress Shoshi, and the two writers were deadly rivals as, indeed, were their mistresses. It is hardly surprising that Murasaki is very rude about Shōnagon, accusing her of frivolity, 'self-satisfaction' and a tendency to 'give free rein to one's emotions'. Alas no other information has survived to balance or qualify such remarks, and we are forced instead to find the 'real' Shōnagon in small details within her own *Pillow Book*, in lines such as 'The face of a child drawn on a melon; wild pinks' (on the list of 'Adorable things').

The same is true of her gardens. While never described in detail they are ever-present, as much a part of the atmosphere as the palace walls and inhabitants: 'I also like frost on a shingle roof or in a garden' (on the list of 'Things that Fall from the Sky'). We hear the rain on the leaves and smell the flowers; we touch petals with Shōnagon's fingers, sensing some of the wonder people felt for the small details of the natural world, albeit heavily controlled by the palace gardeners. Court life was formal, but that did not necessarily make it unpleasant. Shōnagon particularly enjoys the seventh day of the first month 'when people pluck the young herbs

We hear the rain on the leaves and smell the flowers; we touch petals with Shōnagon's fingers, sensing some of the wonder people felt for the small details of the natural world

that have sprouted fresh and green beneath the snow', while, on the third day of the third month, the willows are 'most charming with the buds still enclosed like silkworms in their cocoons'.

The lines between garden and interior are often blurred. For instance, she writes: 'It is a great pleasure to break off a long, beautifully flowering branch from a cherry tree and to arrange it in a large vase'. The vase is by the balustrade of the veranda, neither inside nor out.

Japanese reverence for flowering trees was just as strong in the Heian period as it is today. Plum blossoms 'fill me with happiness', she writes, while 'by the end of the fourth month the orange trees have dark green leaves and are covered with brilliant white flowers'. Like the diarist Samuel Pepys, part of Shōnagon's charm lies in her candour. She used to find pear blossom prosaic, she admits, comparing it to 'thc face of a plain woman', but has changed her mind after examining a single flower in depth, finding a pink tinge so faint she isn't sure if it was there or not. The *Paulownia* tree is not delightful, it is magnificent. The melia tree is 'ugly' but its flowers are 'very pretty indeed'. Everything relates to her personal experience: 'I can never be indifferent to anything that is connected with some special occasion or that has once moved or delighted me'.

Festivals were – and are – often associated with plants, from irises and cherry blossom to lotus and plum. The spring festival of Kamo or Aoi Matsuri began in the sixth century and continues in Kyoto today, celebrating the hollyhock (actually a form of bistort). Hollyhocks are

everywhere, decorating people's homes and headdresses. Finding a dried flower months later may provoke similarly nostalgic emotions now as those felt by Shōnagon a millennium ago.

We learn some of the gardens' geography through unrelated gossip. 'I saw Yukinari, the Controller First Secretary engaged in a long conversation with a lady near the garden fence by the western side of the Empress's office,' tattles Shōnagon, unwittingly revealing something of Japanese garden boundaries in the gossip. Romantic affairs were prohibited but common, and highly ritualized. For Shōnagon, summer was best for such liaisons 'since all the lattices have been left open, one can lie and look out at the garden in the cool morning air' (despite the sexual license of the period, high-class women usually lived behind screens). 'There are still a few endearments to exchange,' she continues, before admitting that usually at such intimate moments, a squawking crow will fly past, shattering the atmosphere. Etiquette required the man to send a note to the lady the morning after; she would respond in kind. The currency was poetry, both in private and public, and a well-turned ode could heal all ills. After one falling out with the other ladies, Shōnagon refuses to return to court, despite Lady Saishō tempting her with reports of the peonies on the Empress's terrace. She is eventually pacified only by a beautifully wrapped, single mountain rose petal, on which the Empress has written the first line of a cherished poem.

Other occasions are more light-hearted. Shōnagon and her friends build a 'snow mountain' in the garden. She loves it so much she bribes a

## We watch with her, delighted, as the morning progresses and the plants spring back into life

gardener to keep it from being kicked over by the rest of the courtiers. The poor man fails; it is never quite clear how much the Empress herself had to do with the mountain's mysterious disappearance.

Shōnagon is not, of course, a hands-on practitioner, but she does worry about how the garden will look. She notes, for example, that in preparation for a festival on the twentieth day of the second month, the cherry blossom is made of paper. The artificiality does not worry her, she admires its artistry, but after a heavy rainstorm the flowers look terrible, like 'the faces of tearful lovers forced to say goodbye'. In a scene straight out of *Alice's Adventures in Wonderland* (see pages 28–33) a team of gardeners is sent to remove the sagging paper blossoms overnight. The Empress quickly cottons on but luckily sees the funny side. No heads are removed.

While often funny, Shōnagon is at her best when writing of beauty. Ten centuries on, we can imagine the clear morning in the ninth month that inspires her 84th stanza. It has been raining all night long as we wake with her and venture into the garden. We see the dew still dripping from the chrysanthemums, picture the bamboo fences and criss-cross hedges of early autumn laced with 'tatters of spider webs', their 'threads broken', raindrops hanging 'like strings of white pearls'. We watch with her, delighted, as the morning progresses and the plants spring back into life, we rush with her to tell everyone how beautiful it all is, then feel with her, crushed, realizing that the most impressive thing of all is that they are not impressed. A thousand years on, none of us can quite convey the loveliness of a garden to someone who has not seen it for themselves.

# Strange Worlds

'The plant was quite well developed before any of us bothered to notice it'

*The Day of the Triffids*, John Wyndham, 1951

Triffids became a byword for any gigantic, terrifying-looking plant almost from the day they were 'released' in 1951 in John Wyndham's *The Day of the Triffids.* Homicidal, exponentially increasing and, most horrible of all, perambulatory, these botanical monsters are only an escaped by-product of the chaos created after an apparent meteor shower renders most of the population blind, but they hit something primeval in our collective imagination. Not only does Wyndham tap into an underlying, existential fear that plants could 'go bad', but he also suggests that the transformation could be the result of human intervention. Very few of us recall the meteor, we all remember the triffid.

Science fiction does not often use plants as main features, but where it does, they are memorable. H.G. Wells was responsible for one of the first, 'The Flowering of the Strange Orchid'. The 1894 short story takes a sly potshot at the Victorian obsession for hothouse orchids, obvious candidates for horror thanks to their otherworldly, alien-like appearance. Poor Winter Wedderburn. He might have chosen any number of innocuous hobbies, collecting stamps, perhaps, or translating Horace. Instead, he innocently purchases the ugliest orchid rhizome in the sale ('like a spider shamming dead' shivers the housekeeper) then becomes its slave. As he obsessively tends it, even with his own blood, in an ecstasy of idol worship, we are brought to mind of another, more famous blood-sucker, Audrey II in Roger Corman's 1960 B-movie *Little Shop of Horrors*. This is not surprising, since it has been suggested that the film (later reinvented as a musical) was

## Science fiction does not often use plants as main features, but where it does, they are memorable

inspired by Arthur C. Clarke's 1956 short story 'The Reluctant Orchid', which was in turn heavily influenced by Wells.

Wells would return to sinister plants in *The War of the Worlds* (1898). This time we tend to remember tripods rather than plants, but Wells tells us that the pernicious red weed the Martians brought with them, perhaps by accident, perhaps design, is what gives the planet its sickly red colour. Stubby-fingered, growing up to nearly two metres (six feet) tall and engulfing whole houses, it is hard to know just how 'evil' the red creeper is – it may be invasive by nature rather than sentient design, but its eventual retreat works well as a literary bellwether, proving that the general threat to Earth is subsiding.

The horrific inkvine is one of several unwelcoming-sounding plants, just one life-form of so many hazards in Frank Herbert's dystopian *Dune* novels (from 1965). Its long tendrils are used as whips in the slave pits of Giedi Prime; anyone touched by them is marked by excruciating, deep red weals forever more.

Herbert's is not an ideal world for a wildlife-watching holiday, but few worlds in science fiction are. Yet, as climate change creeps closer, things seem to be changing for the fantasy botanist. Sue Burke's *Semiosis* (2018) sees colonists on a new planet learn to work with the intelligent plant that controls it. Perhaps there is hope yet for outer space plant–human harmony.

# The Lipton Street Maze

## *Larry's Party*
Carol Shields, 1997

*'A circling, exquisite puzzle of pain, and pain's consolation'*

Larry Weller is a regular guy. He didn't plan to be working for Flower Folks, 'the chain with a social conscience', he only chose floristry because the leaflet about training in furnace repair his mother sent off for turned out to be for a floral art diploma. He is a man of habit; he loves his girlfriend Dorrie and he likes normality. His first act of the novel – accidentally stealing a Harris Tweed jacket – ends with him stuffing the garment in the trash rather than be caught wearing it or facing the embarrassment of returning it.

The turning point in Larry's life comes on his honeymoon, another part of his life he didn't plan. His parents have sent him and Dorrie on a coach tour of Britain. He doesn't immediately 'get' England. Carol Shields subtly makes the tour stop in Saffron Walden, famous for its mazes, but only take 'a quick march through the old, twisted streets'. Gradually, however, Larry begins to fall in love with hedges, unknown in his native Canada. Dorrie loses interest very quickly and even brings up his new obsession in their first argument, claiming that all he cares about is his 'bushes'.

Larry's visit to Hampton Court Maze is a watershed. He gets lost inside and from now on, labyrinths will rule Larry's life.

Carol Shields is probably best known for her novel *The Stone Diaries*, which is about a seemingly ordinary woman. She was keen to write next about what it meant to be a man in the late twentieth century. After encountering a turf maze in Saffron Walden, Shields became a little obsessed with mazes herself, and if the section in *Larry's Party* where Larry goes 'mazing' around the UK and Europe reads a little like a tourist gazetteer, there is good reason: she herself was dazzled by the intricacies of mazes and labyrinths.

Larry and Dorrie buy a fixer-upper house in Lipton Street, Winnipeg, and, under the guise of making the yard safe for their infant son, Larry begins building a hedge maze of his own. His father once had an article about his corkscrew collection in the local newspaper. How fine would it be for Larry's maze to attract similar acclaim?

Time moves on and Dorrie wants to move into a new house with proper railings, in the more upmarket Lipton Wood. Larry is horrified. Every inch of the yard is now covered with miniature hedges that have taken an age to get this high. He cannot bear to start again; besides there might be byelaws that prevent it in Lipton Wood. Only at the end of the chapter do we discover that he is silently worried about the growing distance between him and his wife. Larry has 'shrub mania', Dorrie says, claiming he wants to be 'the shrub king of the universe'.

Larry learns the difference between a labyrinth – with a single path, made for contemplation – and a maze, created to baffle or puzzle. He hardly hears Dorrie's perhaps-joking threat to bring in the bulldozers.

He has just seen what his maze looks like from above from a neighbour's window, and he is in love.

Part of Sheilds's literary skill is in being able to portray two sides of an obsession: both the obsessed and the people who have to live with them. Indeed, she claimed 'this primordial plot of birth, love, work, decline and death' was the only plot she was interested in writing. When Larry's neighbour calls to tell him that Dorrie has finally carried out her threat; that a bulldozer has already dug up part of Larry's beloved maze, his 'piercing cries and howls' are just that: primordial.

Over the next 13 years Larry will pick himself up, become a famous landscape designer, remarry and, at the end of the book, hold that eponymous party. Everything he does will be infused by the Lipton Street garden he left behind in 1983, but for most of the book we know very little about it. We do learn that Larry is now in a one-bedroom apartment, but Shields deliberately leaves the fate of his wounded hedge-maze raw and open, much like Larry himself.

When someone called Big Bruce declares an interest in Larry's designing a maze for Winnipeg without the need for a contract the reader immediately conjures red flags. Shields's style means we learn about events in a strange order, and Big Bruce's maze is temporarily forgotten. Suddenly it is 1986 and Larry's life is completely different. He has left his job and remarried to someone we have not encountered before despite him meeting so many red herrings. Surprisingly, Big Bruce has been as good as his word. The Winnipeg maze is so successful Larry has been commissioned to build another in Chicago. He has also moved house.

Larry's 'historical' house in Oak Park, Illinois, is likely to be at least partly autobiographical. Carol Shields was born in the Chicago suburb, and lived there during her formative years, without ever knowing the windy city itself. She considered her community parochial, conservative, churchgoing. Larry does not seem happy there. The closest he comes to a spiritual experience is on entering an unknown maze for the first time, but otherwise he appears stifled. He cannot even fantasize about building a maze for himself in a place like this. His best idea is to let the garden go wild, but he fears the residents' committees he would horrify if he did. We are reminded that Larry, from blue-collar stock, is now working among the super-wealthy, the only people who can afford the labyrinths he loves.

## The closest he comes to a spiritual experience is on entering an unknown maze for the first time

He negotiates his own maze of memories and people on a daily basis, often finding himself wanting. He now regards that first maze at Lipton Street to be 'crude', something to be embarrassed about and now we finally find something of what happened to it. Despite being easily able to afford to move, despite her shame of the feature, Dorrie still lives there. She has kept the broken hedges – thanks to the bulldozer it now has multiple entrances – and even has them trimmed twice a year. Larry remembers taking his young son round it one evening and berates himself for not then considering himself the luckiest man in the world. He and Dorrie never speak of the maze; 'an exquisite puzzle of pain and pain's consolation'.

We learn of his various commissions, surely the delighted products of Shields's own imagination. We watch his dismay at the nouveau-riche clients who, instead of benches or classical statues, want a barbeque at the centre of their maze. The Saskatchewan maze of hay bales is popular but made of dead material. Larry is not fond of it until later, when he has to make a Great Snow Maze in Ulan-Ude, Sibera, which has so little life he yearns for the straw again. His professional recognition is now commonplace. The Barnes Maze is, the *Chicago Tribune* claims, 'a triumph in contemporary design'. Larry rejected the idea of a fountain at its centre as 'you have to feel doubly lost' in a maze, with barriers both physical and in sensation. Perhaps he is in a maze of his own. At night he experiences insomnia, flipping through a mental portfolio of his completed projects, always finally returning to that first maze at Lipton Street.

He now mainly remembers it in terms of the conflict between himself and Dorrie.

A crack appears in Larry's second marriage when Beth, an academic, applies for a Guggenheim Fellowship and fails to get it. Larry has quietly done the same thing, and succeeds. She sees his actions as underhand; he is keen to help her get over her disappointment. His method is not guaranteed for success: a tour of European mazes. Disappointment looms for both – the Irish Hollywood Stone has been moved to a museum and lost its power, the Hampton Court Maze now seems unsophisticated and banal. As they visit Leeds Castle, Larry tells Beth 'A maze is a machine with people as its moving parts'. She asks, 'Do we want to be part of a machine?'; he is adamant – yes, that way 'we get to be part of the art'. She seems less convinced.

We discover Larry's second marriage has failed as the furniture is sold. At just 45 years old, Larry feels his brain cells collapsing with age.

Carol Shields tells us 'Unless your life is going well you don't dream of giving a party'. Now seemingly recovered, Larry's career is thriving. A small maze he considers his most creatively important will soon be opened. He decides to hold a dinner party with his new girlfriend and does not tell either of his ex-wives that the other will be present.

The final part of the novel deals with Larry's Party, and while not mentioned in the conversation, the Lipton Street maze looms like a phantom over the guests.

At the end of the novel Dorrie asks if Larry really was lost in the Hampton Court Maze on their honeymoon all those years ago. 'I wanted to be lost,' he replies.

# The Garden of Dr Giacomo Rappaccini

## 'Rappaccini's Daughter'
Nathaniel Hawthorne, 1844

*'Many a young man in Padua would give gold to be admitted among those flowers'*

Gardens do not come more Gothic than Nathaniel Hawthorne's lethal Paduan wonderland, locked away and guarded jealously by its sinister creator, Dr Giacomo Rappaccini. Similar in style and planting to the world's first university botanical garden, also in Padua, it is unclear whether the action takes place in that period or some other age. All we know is that it was 'a long time ago'. The garden is clearly beautiful, but from the start there is something strange about it.

We first glimpse it through the eyes of lonely young student Giovanni Guasconti, melancholy in a garret next door. Enticed to look out from his 'high and gloomy chamber' by the old servant Elizabetta, he is enchanted, perhaps in more ways than one. For all its splendour, the garden has fallen on hard times. Its central marble fountain is smashed. Plants creep 'serpent-like' along the ground, others wreathe themselves around statues, veiling them, shrouding them, suggesting darker things found in such wrappings. Nevertheless, water gushes from the spring and many plants are jewel-like in their splendour. One, 'a profusion of purple blossoms', catches Giovanni's eye.

Elizabetta tells him the garden belongs to a 'famous doctor' who distils the plants into medicines. An emaciated, sallow figure in black, Rappaccini seems to be fashioned more along the lines of Doctors

Frankenstein, Jekyll and Moreau than a caring medical practitioner. He enjoys no intimacy with his horticultural charges, donning thick gloves and even a mask when approaching them, before shrinking away and calling out: 'Beatrice!'

Nathaniel Hawthorne is generally associated with the Romantic movement, but his is a dark romanticism with an uneasy moral ambiguity, more akin to writers like Edgar Allan Poe. Hawthorne himself is similarly complex, from complex stock – a line of notoriously harsh Salem judges, one of whom presided over the famous witch trials. Adding a 'w' to his birthname 'Hathorne', perhaps to distance himself from his ancestors, 'Hawthorne' enjoyed his new moniker. A semi-comic 'introduction' to 'Rappaccini's Daughter', supposedly penned by an anonymous academic, critiques the oeuvre of one 'Monsieur de l'Aubépine' (French for 'hawthorn'). The anonymous academic is, of course, Hawthorne himself, but the 'literature critic' framing device is unsettling, much like his story.

If Rappaccini is the crazed scientist of Gothic fiction, his daughter is the genre's damsel in the ruined tower. For a Dante scholar like Giovanni, even her name, Beatrice, signals romance. Innocent, light-hearted, a prisoner in her own garden, she captivates the student spying on her from his window. Even as a drop falls from the stem of a flower she has just picked, accidentally killing a lizard; even when she sighs for an insect that has perished from inhaling her breath, he cannot take his eyes from her.

Giovanni's genial host, Signor Pietro Baglioni, professor of medicine at the university, changes his manner on the mention of Rappaccini: 'He cares infinitely more for science than for mankind,' he warns, but Giovanni is snared. He throws a bouquet of 'good and healthful' flowers down to the object of his affection, unfazed that she has just spoken to the mysterious purple plant as her 'sister'. He tells himself he is probably mistaken when he sees the posy begin to wilt in her hand.

Hawthorne does not appear to have been much of a gardener. A New Englander, he chiefly remembered Maine's 'primeval woods', though in a *National Review* article of 1853, spoke of rolling on a grass plot under an apple tree and picking currants in his grandfather's Salem garden. His seeming indifference to gardening may have partly sprung from his experiences at Brook Farm, a transcendentalist experiment in utopian living that he briefly joined in 1841. His job was to shovel manure.

Mithridatism – regularly ingesting small amounts of poison in order gain immunity – has been a folkloric theme for centuries, notably by the Vishakanya in ancient Indian Sanskrit literature. These 'poison maids' ingested toxins over many years, rendering them deadly to others, ideal honey-trap assassins. In trying to warn Giovanni that he is becoming the subject of one of Rappaccini's experiments, Signor Baglioni tells him of 'an old classic' where such a woman was sent to seduce Alexander the Great. The reader, already suspecting Rappaccini of trialling his poisonous plants as modes of assassination, begins to realize that he has also been drip-feeding his daughter with the garden's lethal harvest.

While it is unclear whether the ancient Vishakanya were complicit in their roles as killers, Beatrice is an innocent. Connected from birth with the garden's unnamed but deadly plants, she considers them her family. Giovanni eagerly accepts Elizabetta's offers to sneak him inside the walls, hardly noticing that Beatrice, while reciprocating his feelings, never allows him to touch either the plants or herself.

Rappaccini seems to be a classic villain. Yet he claims he created this poisoned paradise to protect his daughter, that she might find happiness and a worthy suitor. Most of all, that she might avoid a miserable fate as a 'weak' woman, 'exposed to all evil and capable of none'.

Who then, *is* Hawthorne's guilty party? Some have suggested this is a fable about daring to play God – but who exactly is doing that? Rappaccini, who makes a Garden of Eden for his creation 'Eve', then supplies her with an 'Adam'? Giovanni, tempted by Elizabetta, so disgusted by Beatrice's 'affliction' he goads her into drinking an antidote? The drug's supplier, Professor Baglioni? He, too, is playing with power, a puppeteer pulling Giovanni's strings, perhaps primarily due to professional jealousy.

Hawthorne leaves his characters' culpability ambiguous. Instead, the ending reminds us of another great tragedy. With her dying breath, Beatrice sounds much like Shakespeare's Juliet, claiming she 'will pass away like a dream – like the fragrance of these poisonous flowers, which will no longer taint my breath among the flowers of Eden'. Her Romeo looks on helplessly, only too aware that the garden has nothing to do with Paradise. As Signor Baglioni shouts 'in a tone of triumph, mixed with horror', the two characters that most spring to mind are not Juliet and Romeo, but their two warring father figures, Capulet and Montague.

# Yugiri

## *The Garden of Evening Mists*
Tan Twan Eng, 2012

*'On a mountain above the clouds once lived a man who had been the gardener of the Emperor of Japan'*

Novel openings do not get more fairytale-like than the first line of *The Garden of Evening Mists*, but do not be fooled. There is nothing archetypal or clear-cut about either the romance or the characters within its pages. Heroes and villains are three-dimensional here, with all the messiness that real people bring to fairytales. The garden at the epicentre of this enigmatic, often distressing study on the brutality of war, is equally compromised. Even ruined it is beautiful, but as a masterwork of *shakkei* – the art of borrowed scenery – nothing is entirely what it seems.

The master that created this injured paradise is Nakamura Aritomo, artist, archer and, it is rumoured, once gardener to the emperor until an alleged falling out and self-imposed exile in the late 1930s. After years of wandering Nakamura built his last garden, Yugiri, in Malaya (now peninsular Malaysia), a country savagely treated during the Japanese Occupation between 1941 and 1945.

It is now 1951 and Malaya is in the throes of a new State of Emergency, declared by the British on communist insurgents. Teoh Yun Ling, a Straits Chinese Malayan woman, harbours a hatred for all things Japanese after the three years she and her older sister Yun Hong spent in a forced labour camp. Yun Ling survived, minus some fingers and her childhood; her sister, forced to work as a 'comfort woman', did not. Yet for all their suffering Yun Hong had been obsessed by the beauty of the Japanese traditional gardens of Nakamura Aritomo ever since a family trip to Kyoto before the war, and her descriptions of the fantasy garden they were going to build when they got out kept both girls going.

We learn all this in retrospect, 46 years after Yun Ling first heard Aritomo's name and 34 years after he mysteriously disappeared, 'lost' in a jungle he knew intimately, for *The Garden of Evening Mists* is a Chinese box of a novel, where timeframes nest inside each other, to be constantly unpacked and repacked.

In the modern part of the novel, Malaya's second-ever female Supreme Court Judge Teoh Yun Ling is taking early retirement and finally returning to Yugiri after many years. It is monsoon season; she travels through steamy forests and sodden tea estates into the mists clinging to the mountains. Yugiri's high walls are blotched with moss and old water stains. Ferns sprout from their cracks. She wanders through the overgrown garden, guided by memory, taking a few wrong turns. She passes six tall stones, a miniature mountain range. A pavilion, a pond, a gravel garden.

Yun Ling confides to her equally old friend Frederik Pretorius that she is suffering from aphasia. She has a year, perhaps less, before she loses her senses entirely and she is terrified of losing her story. Frederik tells her to write it down. Later that night she walks Yugiri's paths alone, noting the poorly clipped hedges, the unswept leaves, dead insects and bark peelings, the stone lanterns swathed in spiders' webs and self-seeded ferns. A Buddha's head is 'smoothed by mist and rain'. She reflects that the garden was designed to look old but now it really does. Yes, she must write down her tale. The Chinese box reopens.

Born in Penang and raised in Kuala Lumpur, Tan Twan Eng is himself of Straits Chinese descent, but he does not have a background in gardening. In a 2023 interview, he revealed he is child of the city, not even visiting parks very often. The family was constantly on the move, so books became his friends. He admits to feeling uncomfortable in 'wild' nature, which is perhaps a reason why he was drawn to the formality of Japanese gardens. 'You can have order and nature at the same time,' he suggests. This is possibly why Yugiri's walls are so high, and the rainforest outside is so hostile.

As ever more intricate caskets are unpacked from the novel's nested boxes, we realize that not just gardens are deceptive

Tan once met a former gardener for the Emperor of Japan, along with his brother, also a gardener, working in Johannesburg. Despite the brevity of the meeting, he later watched the brother working with a team of apprentices, pruning and pollarding trees using traditional methods, the epitome of 'order, tranquillity, harmony, neatness and tidiness'. He does not admit in the interview that the encounter was his inspiration for *The Garden of Evening Mists*, but it clearly made a profound impression on him.

In the 1950s, Yun Ling has asked old family friend Magnus Pretorius (Frederik's father) to introduce her to the novel's imperial gardener. She has hardened since her internment, becoming an assistant in the War Crimes Tribunal, ostensibly to find the location of her sister's grave but also from a desire for revenge. The evening before she meets Nakamura, she looks out from Pretorius's veranda towards Yugiri; the garden's fir trees are silhouetted like pagodas in the failing light. The next morning the spell is broken as steaming jungle odours wrench her back to the horrors of her concentration camp.

Searching for a suitable location for his fictional Yugiri, Tan Twan Eng found only two Malaysian regions with a climate conducive for a Japanese garden. He chose the wild/semi-wild landscape of the Cameron Highlands, where the density of the rainforest meets the mystery of the mountains and uniformity of seemingly endless tea plantations, all scarred with a dark history of colonialism, occupation and civil war.

Yun Ling is bleakly impressed that Aritomo (Nakamura's given name, which she uses throughout) does not apologize for the actions of his

countrymen, that he realizes that nothing he could say could atone for the death of her sister or the scars Yun Ling herself still bears. She is stung, however, when he refuses her request to design a garden in her sister's memory. To her astonishment, one week later, the taciturn Aritomo offers something better: to take her on as an apprentice, that she may learn to design her own garden. She will learn with him until the monsoon.

Armed with a book the master has translated into English, Yun Ling learns the history and theory of gardening, of temples in China, of poetry and folklore and literature, of how Japanese gardens slowly evolved their own codes and traditions, and of the romance within such formality, but in the real garden she is given the hard, labouring work. She is instructed not to make notes. 'The garden will remember it for you,' Aritomo tells her, also making her remove her gloves ('What kind of gardener will you be if you do not feel the soil with your bare hands?') revealing the mangled remains of her hands from the attentions of a prison guard. Violence is never far away; guerillas hide in the jungle outside the walls. Yet Yun Ling is calmer for the first time since her incarceration, even if she is 'living the life that should have been my sister's'.

When she first learns about *shakkei*, Yun Ling considers the idea of 'borrowing landscape' as a form of deception. Aritomo retorts that all gardening is deception. Yet as ever more intricate caskets are unpacked from the novel's nested boxes, we realize that not just gardens are deceptive. In the modern-day we learn that Aritomo holds a strange place in the public imagination, not least because he vanished twice, if

one counts the mysterious years of 'wandering' after he left the emperor's service. He also still carries secrets 34 years after his final disappearance.

Tan, too, withholds the full picture from his reader. For all the evocative language, any description of the garden itself is fleeting, allowing us barely snatched glimpses, as though through the dense evening mists themselves. Tantalized by dripping leaves and cloud-drenched mosses, we are left to wonder specifics of the plants they may belong to, or the true shape or construction of the garden. Brief mentions – an elephant-ear fern, a flash of red bromeliad, the fleeting scent of a newly opened lily – seem to conceal rather than reveal the garden's planting scheme. We are invited instead to smell damp earth, to touch rough stone, to listen to the flap of a bird's wing, to watch the powder of termite-devoured bark.

The monsoon arrives and 1950s Yun Ling should be leaving. Instead, she is introduced to *horimono*, the intensely private practice of full-body tattooing, another of the great traditional arts in which Aritomo is a master. As the rain hammers down outside, she undergoes the agony – and eventually obsession – of having her entire back covered in ink. The pain is exquisite, but never worse than that which she and Yun Hong experienced in the camp, of which we now learn, brutality by brutality, slowly, sickeningly realizing how all the characters' lives in this multilayered novel became intertwined.

Alongside the devastating cruelty, *The Garden of Evening Mists* depicts humanity within both sides in the Japanese Occupation. It is not always comfortable reading, and Tan has suggested that historical novels act as

Any description of the garden itself is fleeting, allowing us barely snatched glimpses, as though through the dense evening mists themselves

starting points for debate on complex subjects. Again and again, he uses the garden as a metaphor to navigate life's impermanence. Aritomo, for example, hates the idea of the Garden of Eden, 'where nothing dies or decays, no one grows old, and the seasons never change. How miserable'. He prefers the idea of a garden as a variety of clocks, each element existing within its own time frame of life and death, that must be appreciated separately to be understood as a whole. Perhaps this is the best way to read *The Garden of Evening Mists*, too, with its many boxes within boxes, each of which needs the other to explain it.

# The Sunk Garden

## *Hallowe'en Party*
## Agatha Christie, 1969

*'Bushes of gorse or Spanish broom – Poirot was not famous for knowing the names of either flowers or shrubs'*

Miss Marple is Agatha Christie's most famous gardener. Again and again we meet her pottering around the flowerbeds at Danemead Cottage or, indeed, the many idyllic, picket-fenced Edens of St Mary Mead, not least because they are a great place to learn gossip. Jane Marple, however, never sees Christie's most memorable garden. It is the urbane Hercule Poirot who is forced to get his tight-fitting patent leather shoes muddy in the pursuit of justice in *Hallowe'en Party*.

One of Christie's last whodunits, the novel was not well-received on publication in 1969. Alongside pace-slowing throwbacks to previous 'greatest hits', she, perhaps unwisely, tries to keep up with the times. Her tried-and-tested but quaint by the 1960s style is littered with everything from long-haired beatniks to recreational drugs, the merits of abolishing capital punishment to the dropping of the eleven-plus exam, television to – shock – lesbians, in the process, it would seem, both alienating her core and irritating any prospective audiences. There's no denying it, the inter-war Queen of Crime discussing snogging teenagers, LSD and 'flower-pot' does feel odd. When one of her characters announces that 'hemp has a nasty smell' it's as though the phrase has been uttered by our collective grandmother's maiden aunt. Time has been kinder, however, than the critics, and while not her most tightly plotted mystery, the basic story of *Hallowe'en Party* is solid.

The action is mainly set at the imaginary Woodleigh Common, 30–40 miles from London near the equally fictional Medchester. The village's houses are mainly named for trees: The Elms, Apple Trees, Pine Crest. The only exception is a large Victorian pile boasting a strange garden: Quarry House. Poirot is unimpressed. To him the idea of a 'quarry garden' is 'ugly', suggesting blasted rock, lorries and roadmaking, all alien to this olde-worlde setting. Modernity is insinuating itself everywhere, however, especially with the young people.

We open with the preparations for a children's Hallowe'en party, complete with apostrophe, the 'old' way of spelling it. We soon learn the village is succumbing to ghastly 'Americanisms'. 'I've never really known the difference between a pumpkin and a vegetable marrow,' complains one mother. Even the date, 31 October, is highlighted, presumably for the reader, reminding us that Halloween was not a big thing in 1960s England. Christie uses botanical imagery to remind us it is before All Souls' Day, when the people of Paris put flowers on graves in yet another 'foreign' custom.

Yet Woodleigh's tweenagers whip themselves into a spooky frenzy over classically British traditions, burning their fingers at snapdragon, gazing into rigged mirrors to 'see' their future husbands and covering themselves in flour trying to slice a sixpence. Even the murder weapon is as British as they come: an apple-bobbing bucket.

Agatha Christie always denied that any of her characters were based on herself, but it is hard not to see her in recurring-character Ariadne Oliver, a crime writer who, while making some decent observations, mostly airs her gripes about the publishing industry, the press and the Inland Revenue. She even has a quirky foreign detective character. We are not fooled. Christie happily includes the odd joke at her own expense – the first time we see Oliver in this outing, it is as two escaped apples roll against her feet 'as though arrested by a witch's hand'. We assume that the 'witch' will be our narrator until she leaves Woodleigh Common's shattered paradise and blunders into Hercule Poirot's immaculate art deco apartment, admitting she needs his expertise.

# As Poirot makes his usual round of interviews, he notes not only the houses and their owners, but their gardens too

Christie's ultimate city-detective is the perfect fish-out-of-water detective for *Hallowe'en Party*. Miss Marple would have been far too comfortable among the straggling, late autumn roses, golden rod and Michaelmas daisies. Poirot's feet hurt, his smart clothes are muddy, his general fitness not what it was, yet this cosy world of gardens and gossip is so alien to him he can see it with a fresh eye. His memories of earlier garden visits give Christie an excuse to rehash some of her old books, especially the *Labours of Hercules* series, surely the most preposterous premise ever invented by a mystery writer.

Poirot's first move is to visit the least-alien part of Woodleigh Common, his old friend Superintendent Spence. Christie cannot resist another small gag. 'May your moustaches never grow less,' declares Spence, in the middle of tending his own garden, immediately following up with 'diabolical weeds'.

Poirot soon learns that in this season of mellow fruitfulness, 'one didn't seem to be able to get away from apples'. As he makes his usual round of interviews, he notes not only the houses and their owners, but their gardens too. He is particularly interested in the Sunk Garden at Quarry House. As he learns of the late Mrs Llewellyn-Smythe's wealth, health and garden obsession, the little grey cells begin to work overtime. He learns of her National Trust tour of Irish gardens, and the young landscape architect 'from Wisley or one of those places' she engaged to put her dreams into practice in the old, abandoned quarry she had bought.

# It has been created less by toil than enchantment. The garden was not forced into submission, it has obeyed

There is no suspicion of foul play surrounding Mrs Llewellyn-Smythe's death. Suffering from a heart condition, she was, Poirot learns, told not to do any 'intensive gardening' but what can you expect from 'an energetic woman who has been an enthusiastic gardener all her life'? As the novel progresses, however, we get the feeling that Mrs Llewellyn-Smythe did not spend much time working her garden after all. Poirot gratefully sinks onto a 'strategically placed' bench and imagines how this autumnal vista might look in springtime. He concludes that it has been created less by toil than enchantment. This garden was not forced into submission, it has obeyed. But whose command?

Agatha Christie loved nothing better than to wander around her own garden, Greenway, near Torquay in Devon, on a promontory above the River Dart. A Torquay native, she had always loved the area; purchasing Greenway with her second husband Max Mallowan in 1938 seemed an obvious move. The couple loved to climb its romantic wooded hillsides, then sit contemplating its many natural pleasures. They did not, however, install many of its features. The Camelia Garden, for example, was planted by Edward Elton in the 1790s and the later Carlyon family added many of the specimen trees, including turkey oaks and tulip trees. The Mallowans may perhaps best be described as tender curators of a venerable space, learning as much as possible about their charge and preserving its beauty with honour and humility.

During the Second World War, Greenway was requisitioned for use by the US Coast Guard. Her London house bombed, her husband posted abroad, Christie retreated to the Bauhaus-inspired Lawn Road Flats *aka* the Isokon building at Belsize Park. Fully restored today, visionary Jack Pritchard's gleaming white, reinforced concrete fantasy is much more to Hercule Poirot's modernist tastes, though he would have disapproved that during Christie's tenure it was painted brown for camouflage. Lawn Road had just one garden – on the roof – to which Christie would only have enjoyed access when visiting the Pritchards, and she was clearly homesick. On her return she threw herself back into Greenway's woodlands and dells. It stayed in the family long after her passing.

For all this, the Sunk Garden in *Hallowe'en Party* is not Greenway. While there are aspects of Christie's garden in there – the wildness, the double-edged privacy – we are perhaps better off following Poirot's memories of Greece and Ireland to find her true inspiration. Perhaps this separation is how she can allow the garden to be lovely but haunted. There was once a murder here, and while the rocks may only be metaphorically stained with blood and everything has been covered over, the fear remains. Lovers avoid the place; it is said to be unlucky.

Poirot is initially impressed with the garden's 'magician'. While at first it seems that handsome, arrogant Michael Garfield was just a 'well-paid slave' it soon becomes clear that he is the visionary, carefully moulding his employer's orders to his own ideas. It was Garfield who knew what the garden would look like in years to come, Garfield that could make it stand out in its natural beauty. Bitter that his horticultural baby was merely 'thrown-in' with the house sale, he is wracked with visions of the council taking it over. His greatest fear is that it will be 'kept up', his perfect fairyland, stalwart of *Home and Gardens* magazine, marred by extra paths and litter bins. It takes the 12-year-old 'dryad or elf-like being' Miranda to draw back the curtain, dragging Poirot through a literal hedge to reveal the workings: compost heaps, dustbins and derelict cucumber frames, and pointing out broken ruins where a fountain once played. In her innocence Miranda still yearns for the wishing well in the wood, whatever the sacrifice needed to find it.

In an echo of Mrs Llewellyn-Smythe's Irish tour, Greenway is now owned by the National Trust. In all honesty, however, we must look to our imaginations to find the Sunk Garden.

# The Sheridan Garden

## 'The Garden Party'
Katherine Mansfield, 1922

*'The Karaka trees would be hidden. And they were so lovely with their broad, gleaming leaves and their clusters of yellow fruit... Must they be hidden by a marquee?'*

It is early summer. The weather is at its peak, the sky at its bluest, with only the faintest haze of gold, and the Sheridan family is at its happiest. The garden where they will hold a party this afternoon, is their haven; nothing can interrupt its genteel pace of life. Of course, there is that unpleasant row of poor people's dwellings just down the road, an awful eyesore, but it is easy enough to blot them out behind the karaka trees.

We are never told the exact location of Katherine Mansfield's modernist coming-of-age fable but those karaka trees give the game away. The Sheridan house is based on Mansfield's own childhood home in a comfortable suburb of Wellington, New Zealand. Her father had bought the land in 1887 on condition that he built 'a good and substantial house', from 'materials of the best description', and he had done just that.

The Sheridans do not do their own gardening – their gardener has been up since dawn, mowing and sweeping the lawns until they 'seem to shine'. Neither, however, are they lawn-snobs – they are perfectly happy to leave flat rosettes of daisy leaves in the grass. This is a garden for non-garden-fanatics, for people that just like 'nice things'. The bushes

This is a garden for non-garden-fanatics, for people that just like 'nice things'

bow down 'as though they had been visited by archangels'; the roses have 'understood that roses are the only plants that impress people at garden parties'. Nothing could possibly go wrong in such a haven.

Laura Sheridan is clearly young, probably not long out of childhood. Her mother has absented herself from the party's organization, demanding instead to be treated 'like an honoured guest', and leaving Laura to deal with the workmen erecting the marquee. In her naivety she is delighted such rough men are so nice, failing to notice them subtly manipulating her decision to have the tent raised in the lily lawn to somewhere easier to work. She mourns the loss of a fine view of the karaka trees with their glossy leaves and yellow fruit but decides that this is the sort of thing that happens – the reader fills in 'in the adult world'. We warm to her gaucheness, trying to order the labourers around with a slice of bread and butter in her hand, and to her sympathy for the people who have to work so that her family might have fun, but the class assumptions she has been tacitly taught are never far from the surface. When she notices one of the men rubbing a little lavender between his finger and thumb and sniffing the results, she is delighted that a working man should do such things.

Called away from the sanctity of the garden, Laura enters the house. Her family is based on Louisa May Alcott's 1868 children's classic *Little Women*. Indeed, even the names are the same. If readers who love Hollywood musicals are also reminded of the (much later) Judy Garland vehicle *Meet Me in St Louis*, they will not be the first. American critic Charles Poore placed Sally Benson, author of the novel the film is based on, as being midway between Mansfield and Dorothy Parker.

On this most perfect day the garden seems to come into the house. It is light and airy; faint breezes blow through, even as the servants softly come and go through the green baize door. Flowers arrive with another tradesman, a florist, to the delight of the family – and the mild consternation of the reader. For these are canna lilies. They may be pink, but in many traditions lilies mean one thing: death. These, on bright crimson stems, are 'almost frighteningly alive'. Laura declares it must be a mistake, but rather than airing any superstitious doubts she is merely surprised at the amount of them.

There is a death in the story, just not the one we might expect. There has been an accident in the village. The dead man is a stranger, from one of those eyesore houses – 'mean little dwellings' where 'the very smoke is poverty-stricken'. Laura, the empath, cannot think how they can possibly have a party now, with a man dead 'just outside the front gate'. What would the widow think, hearing a band playing happy songs? Her sister, while claiming she is sympathetic, hardens her eyes and announces that the man was drunk, something she does not know. When their mother hears the news, her first reaction is 'Not in the garden!'. On discovering it is only in the poor cottages down the road, her relief shocks Laura. She is further upset when she learns the party will go ahead as normal and is told to wear her new hat. Mansfield slyly makes it black, with a gold trim.

The party itself is over in a few lines. We learn of the band, laughed at by a friend for looking like frogs in their livery, but brought refreshments by Laura. We see couples wandering through the garden, admiring the flowers, but Mansfield's treatment of it is almost throwaway.

Laura's embarrassment is palpable when her mother has a 'good idea' and decides to send the leftover party food to the grieving widow. And, while Laura is carrying it over, how about taking those lilies, too, because 'people of that class are so impressed by arum lilies'. Mother is only dissuaded by the thought of the pollen staining Laura's lace dress.

We burn with Laura's shame as she puts her mother's thoughtless 'generosity' into action, offering scraps of celebration food to a woman in pain. Just as she thinks things cannot get any worse, she is ushered in to view the body, and the story takes an unexpected turn.

Katherine Mansfield was suffering from tuberculosis when she wrote 'The Garden Party'. She spent 1922 in Paris undergoing experimental x-ray treatment, but the garden of her childhood called to her. 'I shall have a garden one day,' she wrote to her husband, John Middleton Murry, that October. 'Oh, how I love flowers, I think of them with such longing'.

Mansfield died in Paris in January 1923. She did, however, get her garden. Her New Zealand home, now the Katherine Mansfield House and Garden Museum, has a garden made especially for her, filled with the roses that so impress people at garden parties.

# Literary Plants

'There's a tree that grows in Brooklyn. Some people call it the Tree of Heaven'

*A Tree Grows in Brooklyn*, Betty Smith, 1943

Gardens in literature may be places of contemplation, joy, memory or retreat, but authors have often used individual plants or varieties to lend specific vibrance, emotion and analogy to their worlds.

The deadly poppy fields in L. Frank Baum's *The Wonderful Wizard of Oz,* for example, show how every member of the party must contribute to a quest. The three biological travellers – Dorothy, Toto and the Cowardly Lion – all fall under the heady influence of the poppies' fragrance, needing the help of the two non-biological characters, the Scarecrow and the Tin Man, each of whom have doubted their own self-worth, yet remain immune to the drug.

Far more darkly, the red hibiscus growing in Aunty Ifeoma's garden in Chimamanda Ngozi Adichie's *Purple Hibiscus* reminds us of the constant bloodshed inflicted on the young heroes by their tyrannical father. The eponymous purple variety, however, is a different symbol: 'rare, fragrant, with undertones of freedom'. The 'freedom' Kambili and Jaja eventually find will be deeply compromised but not without hope: they plan to plant their own purple hibiscus as soon as they are able.

Trees hold a particular fascination in literature. Frances Hardinge's sinister *Lie Tree* will only grow strongly if lies are whispered to its roots, but eating the fruits of those lies will reveal a truth about the consumer. The Tree of Heaven in Betty Smith's *A Tree Grows in Brooklyn* was born from rubbish heaps and cellars and gratings, 'the only tree that grows out of cement'. It is, like many of the human residents of Brooklyn, an incomer. Like them, it was once welcomed, but quickly outstayed the hospitality.

# Authors have often used individual plants or varieties to lend specific vibrance, emotion and analogy to their worlds

Now a fast-growing 'invasive alien', it has been eradicated from smart neighbourhoods, but still grows strongly in the poorer districts, symbolizing tenacity and survival. The chestnut tree that the visionary José Arcadio Buendía is tied to by his family in the sprawling *One Hundred Years of Solitude* (Gabriel García Márquez) will also survive, long after José's death, albeit kept company by his ghost.

Part detective story, part comedy of the darkest variety, Percival Everett's satire *The Trees* inverts racial stereotypes to reveal truths behind social justice or, rather, the continuing lack of it. The trees of the title do not just represent the 'strange fruit' lynchings of America (at one point Everett breaks away from the comic character names and knockabout police procedural to list the real-life subjects of racial murders; it takes ten pages) but also plays on the idea of family trees. Horror and revenge in Everett's world are no respecters of the generations.

# Mr McGregor's Garden

## *The Tale of Peter Rabbit*
Beatrix Potter, 1902

*'First he ate some lettuces and some French beans; and then he ate some radishes'*

Once upon a time there were four little rabbits… It is perhaps fitting that one of the world's most famous nursery stories should have a fairytale opening. *The Tale of Peter Rabbit* starts in the woods, the natural world, where four little bunnies live with their mother under a fir tree. In most fairytales, venturing into the forest is the moment where the hero leaves behind any sense of security, to face the dangerous, the unknown. Here, it is the other way around. The scariest place on Earth is a humble vegetable patch, ordered, neat – and lethal.

The first time we see the rabbit family they look like animals children might glimpse in real life: sweet, furry – and naked. Their burrow is warm and safe, but they cannot not stay there. Mother must find food. She tells them to be good and to stay close to home. Fixing her son's little blue jacket collar, she is adamant: do not go anywhere near Mr McGregor's garden. Mother rabbit cannot mince her words, for the sake of her brood. They are a one-parent family because Mr McGregor put their father in a pie. While the good little bunnies pick blackberries in the wood, however, naughty Peter has other ideas.

Gates are always liminal spaces in folklore, and the one Peter squeezes under – a homely wicket-affair, edged with holly, a plant of both woodland and the cultivated garden – would be passed through the other way by any

other hero, leaving civilization to face the wild wood. Peter is not any other hero. This adventurer is of the wild wood himself, and he is about to face his nemesis – an elderly man.

Readers familiar with Beatrix Potter's charming cottage in the English Lake District might be forgiven for assuming that Mr McGregor's garden was based on the author's own. In reality, Potter did not purchase Hill Top until 1905, three years after *Peter Rabbit* was published. Much like her turning the traditional hero story on its head by sending a wild creature into the human world, it is far more likely that Potter's kitchen garden is based on the one she invented for her villain.

Potter was born and raised in London. South Kensington was home to the Natural History Museum, and the young Beatrix was passionate about all things natural. Her intricate botanical illustrations, especially of fungi, are well-respected today but as a Victorian woman she was not taken seriously. Her paper on fungi, submitted to the Linnean Society in 1897, was unsuccessful (female Fellows were fiercely opposed until 1904) so she turned to a much more 'ladylike' outlet for women artists: children's books. *The Tale of Peter Rabbit* was privately printed in 1901 and commercially published in 1902 by Frederick Warne & Co.

Potter may not have entirely invented Mr McGregor's vegetable patch. It is widely suggested she based *The Tale of the Flopsy Bunnies* on her uncle and aunt's walled garden at Gwaenynog in Wales, and Mr McGregor's neat rows of cabbages and beans are typical of nineteenth-century kitchen gardens up and down the land. Potter's detailed

illustrations prove she was familiar with her subject. From the old-fashioned, long variety of radishes Peter consumes when he first arrives in the garden, through rows of French beans and lettuces to the detailed representations of pelargoniums that Peter later knocks over in his haste, it is clear this world has been drawn by someone with a background in botanical illustration.

Potter's familiarity with the process of gardening is also clear. The spade speared into the earth as Peter gobbles his ill-gotten gains reminds us of the human threat. Even the robin cannot save him as, searching for parsley, a traditional herbal remedy for tummy ache, he ventures ever closer to the non-natural: the pots of cane-supported vegetables, the cold frame and, finally, Mr McGregor himself. We first see him on his hands and knees, planting out seedlings in rows, looking like anything but an enemy. He chases Peter with human weapons, a rake, then a sieve, but the most horrific image in the book is not from a deliberate attack.

The image of a rabbit caught in netting is perhaps even more poignant today than it would have been in Potter's time, in that modern, plastic netting is deadly. Happily, Peter's trap is made from twine and his friends the sparrows can release him, but the garden remains an obstacle course. Peter's next hiding place, a watering can, is full. Inside the shed, a place many children would have been familiar with, upturned terracotta pots, a broom, spade and trowel all become potential instruments of torture. Even an ornamental goldfish pond is set with a trap of the feline variety.

As Peter creeps away we glimpse more of Mr McGregor's immaculate potager, complete with low box hedges and regimented cabbages. From a wheelbarrow we gaze with Peter as he yearns for the safety of the forest, only kept at bay by high yew hedges. It is so close, but there is one more barrier to freedom: the old gardener himself, currently hoeing onions.

Potter's skill lies with the Brechtian concept of making the familiar strange, that an audience may view something 'normal' more dispassionately. Her readers would have known kitchen gardens as comforting havens, yet through Peter Rabbit, she shows us that not everyone sees things the same way we do. As Peter scoots through the (cultivated) black*currant* bushes to the safety of the (wild) black*berry* patch, Mr McGregor is already making his clothes into a scarecrow.

Little bunnies have no place in the human world, especially not wearing jackets and shoes.

While the 'good children' get milk and blackberries, Mother Rabbit gives Peter a dose of chamomile tea, presented like a classic Victorian nursery punishment. We do not get the feeling he has learned his lesson.

Beatrix Potter bought Hill Top in the throes of mourning her fiancé, publisher Norman Warne, who had believed in her as much as he had loved her. She poured her grief into the cottage and its garden, especially the vegetable patch. She would eventually marry a solicitor, move to the other side of thc village and even purchase several farms, but she never relinquished her first outdoor space, somewhere she could call her own, somewhere she could became a benign Mrs McGregor.

# Ashoka Vatika

## *Rāmāyaṇa*

Vālmīki, EXACT DATE UNKNOWN

*'In the garden of thy heart, plant naught but the rose of love'*

The *Rāmāyaṇa* is one of two ancient Hindu epic texts (the other being the later but longer *Mahābhārata*). It tells the story of Prince Rāma of the legendary city of Ayodhya (popularly associated with the modern day city in Uttar Pradesh, India), of his life, trials and eventual reign on Earth. Originally written in Sanskrit sometime between the eighth century BCE and the fourth century CE, by the legendary poet Vālmīki, this hugely important story may be found in many cultures including the Buddhist, Sikh and Jain faiths, and there are local variants for most Southeast Asian countries. With so many interpretations (and spellings) it is impossible to pinpoint exact dates, details or even a definitive version, but even today the tale remains fresh, constantly reinvented in plays, books, graphic novels, dance-dramas, art, video games, major TV series and dozens of Bollywood movies.

After winning the Princess Sītā by stringing a magical bow, Rāma, seventh avatar of the god Vishnu, is newly married and about to be granted his rightful crown of Ayodhya when an elderly maidservant reminds the king of a double promise he once made to her. She now claims these boons – to place her own son, Bharata, on the throne and to be rid of Rāma.

Over 24,000 verses, the rightful prince is plunged into a 14-year exile and a life of travel through the forests of the Indian subcontinent – 'Rāmāyaṇa' literally means 'Rāma's journey' – accompanied by his faithful brother Lakṣmaṇa and Sītā, who has refused to stay behind.

The travellers' greatest danger lies with Rāvana, the multi-headed rakshasa (demon) king of Lanka, an island fortress, whose exact location scholars have debated for millennia. On failing to seduce the brothers, Rāvana's sister Shurpanakha tries to kill Sītā, but is stopped by Lakṣmaṇa, who cuts off her nose. Rāvana vows revenge by kidnapping Sītā, which he manages despite the efforts of Rāma's friend Jatāyu the vulture, who is mortally wounded. Setting out to rescue Sītā, Rāma encounters Hanumān the legendary ape general. Jatāyu's brother tells the brothers that Sītā been taken to Lanka and Hanumān offers to be a scout. Assuming massive form, he follows the demon king.

Rāvana's air-chariot Pushpaka Vimana, which resembles a flying peacock, lands in Lanka, where the demon tries to make Sītā his bride via a series of promises and threats. The ultimate Hindu heroine, she refuses to marry him or to stay in his luxurious palace. She chooses instead to stay in the Ashoka Vatika, literally, 'the garden of ashoka trees'.

Sanskrit for 'sorrow-free', *Saraca asoca* is prized for its beautiful pinnate leaves and fragrant, orange flowers. It is still found in temple and palace gardens and is sacred to Kamadeva, the Hindu god of love. Sometimes it is known as Sītā Ashok, symbolizing the princess's undying devoted love for, and faith in, her husband.

In some versions of the tale Sītā sits under a shimsapa tree. Like so many details about the epic, it is not entirely clear which plant this is, or even if it is supposed to be based on a real tree, but some have identified it either as *Dalbergia sissoo,* an Indian rosewood, or *Amherstia nobilis,* a large tropical tree with luxurious flowers.

Just because Rāvana is an evil demon does not mean he is immune to beauty. His fabulous, green vatika is surrounded by sumptuous garden buildings constructed by Vishwakarma, the craftsman deity mainly responsible for the gods' chariots. In some versions he is also responsible for the garden itself. The planting is lush, the flowers heady with perfume. Unexpectedly, perhaps, Rāvana's wife Mandodari is not evil. Pious and pure, she loves her rakshasa husband despite his faults, but visits Sītā in the garden and ultimately saves her life by standing up to him.

Hanumān discovers Sītā in the garden and offers to carry her back to her husband. She refuses – it is not 'dharma' to sneak away like that, only shame could come from such unheroic actions. Rāma himself must rescue her and avenge her kidnapping. Hanumān readily agrees, but he is not finished. He destroys the garden's trees and pavilions while allowing himself to be captured, admonishing Rāvana for the abduction. He is condemned to death for his insolence but, his tail on fire, he escapes and leaps across the roofs of the palace, setting fire to everything he sees, including the Ashoka Vatika, laying the groundwork for the final Battle of Lanka. The soil where once the garden flourished turns black, like ash.

While the exact location of Lanka is disputed, there are many place names and shrines celebrating Rāma, Sītā and other characters from *Rāmāyaṇa* on the island of Sri Lanka. Indeed, for Sri Lankan people, Rāvana is not a demon, but a learned scholar and brilliant statesman. In particular, the Sita Amman temple, between the cities of Sita Eliya and Nuwara Eliya, is said to be built on the site of a much older shrine dedicated to Sītā, and to this day, a gigantic 'footprint' shows where Hanumān sank into the ground on landing in the garden. The soil around the area, unlike most of Sri Lanka's rusty-red earth, is black. Nearby, is Hakgala Botanical Garden, created in 1861 by George Henry Kendrick Thwaites as an experimental garden for anti-malaria drugs. It is 1,650 metres (5,400 feet) above sea level but legend holds that the jungle even higher than that covers the land of the fabled Ashoka Vatika.

# The Botanic Gardens, Kew

## 'Kew Gardens'
Virginia Woolf, 1919

*'There rose perhaps a hundred stalks spreading into heart-shaped or tongue-shaped leaves'*

The impressionistic short story 'Kew Gardens' could only have been composed by an author steeped in the natural world. Virginia Woolf's narrative swirls with the romance of the garden, very deliberately part of, not mere backdrop to her pithy pen-sketches of human lives. While the reader is lured by the big picture – the warm July breeze, distant figures diminished in size against the trees – Woolf immediately also plunges us into the microscopic. The soft earth. A raindrop. A throat, from which peeps a bar, 'rough with gold dust' and 'slightly clubbed at the end' taking us deep inside the botanical construction of a flower. She surrounds us with a kaleidoscope of colours: red, blue, yellow, red, blue, yellow, repeated, again and again, dappled with brown, silver-grey, green, all sent scattering into the air above by a sudden gust, to be enjoyed by the men and women who walk through Kew.

The conceit – a sunny afternoon in the Royal Botanic Gardens – sees a role-reversal in viewpoints as a single flower bed becomes witness to a series of fleeting moments in humanity. As a tiny snail begins a small odyssey across 'brown cliffs and deep green lakes' within the bed, people pause, like the butterflies darting around the flowers, leaving us with snatches of conversation. A married man's thoughts wander to a previous visit many years earlier where, if only those dragonflies had

She manages to make Kew at once the realm of the everyman and deeply personal

landed for a second, the girl he begged to marry him might have said yes. His wife Eleanor enjoys different, but equally tender memories, of a kiss on the back of her neck from a beloved, elderly teacher, 'the mother of all my kisses'. They drift on, and an elderly gentleman arrives with visions of his own. Eleanor saw the memories preserved by the gardens as 'ghosts lying under the trees' but the elderly gentleman encourages the spirits of his beloved dead to visit him. He describes an elaborate, battery-powered spiritualist's device but does not need it. He already sees and hears his phantoms here. When his young companion tries to distract him with a flower, the gentleman listens – and replies – to whatever the bloom has said to him. Even a pair of gossipy 'lower middle class' women are momentarily stopped in their chatter by the sight of the flowers, stunned into contemplation before a desire to have tea breaks their reverie.

The snail continues its slow journey, observed with the same minute detail Woolf affords her human subjects, her deft, painterly strokes leaving us to piece together lives from the fragments we are given. For a line or two, 'ordinary' folk are elevated to exotic species. The next couple is young and earnest, each unsure of the other. The young man gauchely remarks that he is glad it is not Friday, or they'd have to pay sixpence admission. His sweetheart asks, 'Is it worth sixpence?' leaving the reader to decide whether she means the entrance cost, or herself. The question hangs for a moment, then they reach the flower bed, his hand touches hers and together they press the end of her parasol into the earth.

Woolf undercuts even this extraordinary moment of understated passion as the girl wonders what kind of tea they give at Kew and the young man feels the two-shilling piece in his pocket. We feel with him the slightest sense of relief as she becomes distracted by the gardens' other charms, including a Chinese pagoda, forgetting the white tablecloths and waitresses that would look 'first at her then at him'.

We are left in no doubt that not only is Kew Gardens a real location, but one that Virginia Woolf knew intimately. Using the practicalities of a visit – the tea rooms, the six-penny entrance fee – she manages to make Kew at once the realm of the everyman and deeply personal.

Virginia and her husband Leonard Woolf had moved into 34 Paradise Road, Richmond, in 1915, naming it Hogarth House. It was close enough to be able to glimpse the Chinese pagoda that distracts the young man's sweetheart from the top floor, and she would have been a frequent visitor to the gardens. It begs a question: were these exquisite snatches of conversation products of her imagination based on Woolf's visits, or real, overheard moments witnessed there?

In 1917, the Woolfs set up a small publishing company in their drawing room, using a tiny manual printing press. By 1946, Hogarth Press had published 527 works and it still exists today as an imprint of Penguin Random House. 'Kew Gardens' was accompanied by a pair of woodcuts by Virginia's sister Vanessa Bell, who had been urging her to write shorter works.

At the end of 'Kew Gardens', the colours return, first as a hazy dream of green, blue, white, yellow, black, pink, red and blue, but now the mist is clearing. A sense of reality nags at the reader. Woolf reminds us there is no real peace from modernity. Omnibuses turn their wheels and change gear, voices cry and, oddest of all, 'the petals of myraids of flowers flashed their colours into the air' in a cacophony of public vibrance. Kew Gardens is not, after all, the retreat Woolf needed.

Happily for her, she was able to get away from it all. Famously part of the Bloomsbury Set of writers, artists and intellectuals, the same year as 'Kew Gardens' was published the Woolfs acquired the garden most associated with them: the one at Monk's House, Rodmell, near to the home of her sister Vanessa at Charleston, on the south coast. Woolf did not immediately care for the house, but she was entranced by the garden and a later story, 'In the Orchard', is heavily inspired by it. Although not a great hands-on gardener (Leonard was the horticultural fanatic), Virginia would eventually move her writing studio outside, and gardens remained a powerful inspiration for the rest of her life.

# Sido's Garden

## *My Mother's House*
## *Sido*
## Colette, 1922, 1929

*'The beak of a secateur goes clicking all down the rose-bordered paths'*

Sidonie-Gabrielle Colette's voracious appetite for life was surpassed only by her outstanding skills with a Parker Duofold fountain pen. Author, actress, journalist, music hall star and *bonne vivante*; three times married along with any number of affairs with men and women, her pleasures were both sensuous and sensual. She adored food as much as – perhaps even more than – sex, describing the curve of a melon or the scent of a tomato with the licentiousness of a lover, regarding the plants they grew on in the same hedonistic spirit. Colette is justly regarded by many as one of the most remarkable women of the twentieth century. She would have disagreed, pointing instead to Adèle Eugénie Sidonie 'Sido' Landoy, the matriarch at the centre of her young world who was nurturing, powerful, taking whatever life threw at her, dealing with it and still drinking deeply from life's cup. Virtually any of Colette's many works might have been chosen for a book about gardens in literature. Flowers, plants and all things that grow are central to her universe. It is in her fictionalized memoirs *My Mother's House* and *Sido,* however, that her gluttony for gardens is most truly sated, via a compelling central figure, that of her mother.

Taking a non-linear, episodic format, *My Mother's House* is based on a 1922 collection of vignettes *La Maison de Claudine*, perhaps to capitalize on the success of the vaguely autobiographical (and, at the time, scandalous)

## We are warm, the early summer air is heady with the scent of tomato leaves and apricots ripening against ancient walls

*Claudine* novels that had catapulted her into early twentieth-century Paris. The titular character does not appear in *La Maison*... which would have disappointed only diehard Claudine fans. *My Mother's House* envelopes every one of the senses from its very first paragraphs, presenting the reader with a Jackson Pollock of Colette's own early life. Characters, ideas, images, sounds, smells, blood, mud, milk and sweat are thrown at her canvas, emotions flicked across the result with the same intensity with which she attacked everything. At the centre of it all, sits Sido, resplendent in faded frock and gardening apron, the beak of her secateurs peeping through a hole in the pocket, a packet of love-in-a-mist seeds rattling like rain when she moves. Yet before we even meet this Amazon, we meet her garden.

Colette's descriptions are precise. The Upper Garden overlooks the Lower Garden, an enclosed potager for aubergines and pimento. We are warm, the early summer air is heady with the scent of tomato leaves and apricots ripening against ancient walls. We see a pair of twin firs, an 'intolerant' walnut tree whose shade kills the flowers struggling beneath it. We learn of rose bushes, 'ruddy festoons of an autumn vine', lilacs 'stifled by their own exuberance', a 'neglected' lawn and 'dilapidated' arbour. This joyful jumble should be private, but the whole village can see in. No one can remember a time when the boundary wall wasn't broken, struggling under 'the invincible arms of a hundred-year-old wisteria'. Like the rest of the novella's characters, the Colette family garden is anything but immaculate, but it is, nevertheless, perfect. Or at least it is in

her memory. The house and garden still exist, we are told, but we must labour under no illusions: the magic has deserted them. 'They once held a family,' say our narrator, 'now they are suddenly emptied of joy'.

All that is to come, however. We first encounter Sido 'small and plump in those days when age had not yet wasted her'. We meet the author's father, the single-legged Captain Colette, her siblings and neighbours, getting to know them via often trivial incidents – moths in the captain's cloak, blackbirds in the cherries, butterflies, grass snakes, kittens. Sido cheerfully multitasks children's tea preparation, dog-washing, skinned-knee tending and laundry even as she manages her chaotic but productive garden. We see her as an 18-year-old, whisked away by 'The Savage', the descendant of a distantly noble family, despite her dowerless, trousseau-less, jewel-less state, chosen for her sheer *joie de vivre*. Swapping her comfortable Belgian home for an isolated country house, she fills it with flowers, turns it into a home, then becomes desperately lonely.

We are not told how she has arrived in the village of Saint-Sauveur-en-Puisaye with the captain, but the real-life Sido was widowed. The couple, who now have children of their own, bicker; Colette, just 15, admits later she 'had not yet divined the ferocity of love beneath his veteran eyebrow and the blushes of adolescence upon her fading cheeks'. Later she will wonder if she knew her father at all.

Sido brings her dog to mass and reads Corneille plays hidden in a prayer book. She ignores neighbours' gossip, delights in the feathers of a bird and adores her family. She notices everything but allows each member the space to develop and bloom in their own time, the essence behind her daughter's own values. On noticing how much her youngest daughter loves the dawn, she gets up at three that she might wake her to enjoy it. There, Colette sees a magical kingdom 'slumbering in primal blue', 'blurred and dewy, the mist grounded by its own weight' in which she gathers strawberries, blackcurrants and gooseberries. Sido stays back, allows her daughter to wander alone in 'the free-thinking countryside' where 'I first became aware of my own self'. She is, quite simply, the ideal mother.

We must remember that for all their bucolic charm *My Mother's House* and *Sido* are fictionalized memoirs. We have no way of knowing how factually accurate they may be regarding Colette's childhood. That does not make them any less true. Her memories – of her mother's 'fragrant' gardening frock, of a garden where the tobacco plants 'open to the night', where 'a ray of light strikes the walnut tree releasing the bitter, cool smell of the worm-eaten walnuts fallen on the grass' – are so palpable that we *know* they really existed. We just don't know whether they really existed in the world or really existed in her imagination.

In 1925, Colette bought La Treille Muscate, a wisteria-draped villa in Saint-Tropez, not for the quality of the house but for the freedom she might find there, and for the garden she wanted to build, filled with fruit and herbs and roses. In her fifties now, she was beginning to suffer the chronic pain that would haunt her later years, confining her to a couch and eventually to bed. Reminiscences in later books such as *Flowers and Fruit* and *For a Flower Album* specifically discuss plants in depth long after she was unable to physically put trowel to soil, but it is not Saint-Tropez she is dreaming about. As the ageing free spirit potters around various imaginary gardens, thinking about how she would plant-up their different terrains, she is clearly remembering her mother.

Sido has her own secrets to bear. *My Mother's House* darts around timelines, settling briefly, butterfly-like, on individual petals of a life well-lived, but it broadly follows a chronology that is hurtling to a bittersweet ending. Dressed in her nightgown, still small, but now fierce with age, Sido chops wood with a hatchet, draws water from the well, splits firewood with a billhook and attacks the ground with a mattock, defying disease with the 'forbidden fruits' of her formerly active life. Colette wishes she had a photograph with which to illustrate the book. We do not need one.

*My Mother's House* and *Sido* take a melancholy turn as Colette remembers every part of her mother – the sun-warmed walls, the wet, leathery hydrangea leaves, the barbed caterpillars of the monkey puzzle tree – for the garden *is* her mother. A woman who can 'evoke the wind at will' to 'rustle the stiff, papery blades of the bamboos'. We can smell the crushed grass, hear Sido's secateurs clicking down the rose paths, see the 'puffs of smoke' plum trees, feel the 'unicorn tips' of the lords-and-ladies, taste the last of the black cherries.

Rose-tinted spectacles removed, Colette's loosely autobiographical 'memoirs' may seem just a little too bucolic to be entirely believed. How much of this idyllic life did she actually live? Yet the garden, plants, animals and people she describes embody a life we *want* her to have lived. Above all, we want a mother like Sido, we want her to have been exactly who she was, even if the pleasure also involves desperate heartbreak along the way. For this is a book to be read through a glassy film of tears, one's whole body aching for that 'something' most of us fail to articulate but which flowed so effortlessly from Colette's Parker pen onto her trademark blue manuscript paper.

# Barchetto del Duca

## *The Garden of the Finzi-Continis*
Giorgio Bassani, 1962

*'How beautiful Barchetto del Duca was at night, I said to myself, how sweetly it lay in the moonlight'*

A high wall. A secret garden. A princess, waiting to be kissed. Giorgio Bassani's mid-twentieth-century blockbuster could be an Italian fairytale if it wasn't for the gas chambers.

We know from the start of this apparently romantic yarn of missed opportunities that none of the Finzi-Continis survived the Second World War. Years later, as our anonymous narrator visits some Etruscan tombs, he is reminded of the great family's mausoleum at the Jewish cemetery of his (and Bassani's) home city, Ferrara. Where the people he knew are buried, however, 'is anyone's guess'.

Bassani is not an experimental author, but he does use footnotes, call his prologue a 'foreword' and dedicate the book to his main female character, implying his book is a memoir, a work of non-fiction. There is, undeniably, a large part of Bassani in the work. Born into a prosperous Jewish family and attending university in 1938/9 as the infamous race laws were introduced by Mussolini's fascists, he knew the people of Ferrara's ghetto, saw first-hand the destruction of a community that had existed since 1277. *The Garden of the Finzi-Continis* is, however, very definitely fiction, and no part of the novel is more invented than the garden itself.

Ferrara is an ancient walled city in Emilia Romagna, Northern Italy, but the Finzi-Contini's 'endless wall', their 'dark oak gate without any handles at all or else on the other side', their 'woody trunks and branches' and 'strange spiky outline of the house' are pure fantasy. Indeed, the great park does not even last to the end of the novel. Bassani spends an entire paragraph tenderly listing the varieties of tree razed by the fascists; all that is left now is bare, broken soil.

*The Garden of the Finzi-Continis* is the most famous in a series of novels, later bound as a single volume, *Il Romanzo di Ferrara* (*The Novel of Ferarra*). The books explore often marginalized lives, including those of homosexual characters and, especially, the Jewish community. Ferrara's ghetto is depicted as a tiny world within a world. The wealthy and cultured Finzi-Continis keep even further to themselves. After the death of a son, Guido, the two subsequent children, Alberto and Micòl, have been privately educated and are seen only at a distance in synagogue. Our narrator, their contemporary, occasionally whispers with Alberto, but glimpses his sister Micòl only from a distance, sequestered with the women.

He is first presented with a chance to see behind the high Finzi-Contini walls in 1929. After failing an exam at school, he runs away, and eventually finds himself in a dappled umbrella of branches, the same venerable trees that will be sacrificed as firewood 12 years later during 'the freezing winter of Stalingrad'. But that is for the future. Today, the sky is blue, 'without a trace of cloud'. He is surprised to hear a voice. Thirteen-year-old Micòl is watching him from the top of the wall, standing on a

# The garden becomes a little ghetto in itself, a haven from the outside world

ladder the other side. She invites him to join her, but he is afraid. She nimbly scampers down to show him the footholds, but he again demurs, afraid for the security of his new bicycle. She tells him to hide it in an old artillery store. As he does so, he imagines kissing her, but by the time he reemerges she is gone. He has missed his moment and will not get another for nearly ten years.

It is November 1938, two months after new racial laws have barred Italy's 46,000 Jews from an extraordinary range of occupations from teaching to medicine, publishing to government. Like Bassani himself (he was cast out of his tennis club in 1938), Jews have also been expelled from sports memberships. Alberto Finzi-Contini invites our storyteller to play tennis on his family's private court, inside those famous walls.

The narrator joins Alberto, Micòl and several other expelled club members, and the garden becomes a little ghetto in itself, a haven from the outside world, however illusory the sensation of safety might be. Despite the late month, the weather is perfect. It feels like summer, but it is 'too glorious'. Like children stumbling into the forbidden land of the fairies, the young people are plied with delicacies and urged to stay. They play tennis and enjoy the once-forbidden garden across a black girder bridge, over the canal and through an arch of roses.

It is often suggested that the inspiration for this imaginary paradise was a garden several hundred kilometres away. Ninfa, in Latina, central Italy, has been called 'the world's most romantic garden'. Created by the Caetani family from 1921, the ruined medieval town was transformed over the middle years of the twentieth century into an enchanting confection of roses, turrets and running waters. Bassani knew both garden and owners intimately; it seems plausible, likely even, that it also enjoys an alternative life as the great park of the Finzi-Continis.

Micòl offers to show our narrator around the garden, by bicycle, for it is fully ten hectares in size, with six kilometres of paths. The pair banter, bicker and watch the trains shunting at the railway station, perhaps reminding us of how Ferarra's Jews will eventually leave the city. They talk about trees, stopping by an American aloe 'shaped like the candelabra of the menorah' which flowers only once at around 20 or 25 years old, then dies. Micòl shows him the wall where they first met, where she placed the ladder, then suggests erecting a small commemorative plaque to the incident. He laughs; we think of other places where memorial plaques are mounted, remembering that Micòl does not have one and that we do not yet know what happened to her. She tells him she never asked anyone else into the garden; he fantasizes about kissing her. Is she giving him ample opportunity to do so, or is/was this just his imagination? One day she takes him into the coach house. It is filled with ripening fruit. Nothing happens, and the following day she goes to Venice.

Our narrator spends more time with Alberto and when he is ejected from the public library, Alberto's father, Professor Ermanno allows him to use his private book collection. 'Whenever the door was open we even exchanged a few words,' he tells us. '"What's the time,' 'How's the work going'" and so on. A few years on, he will exchange much the same words with the inmate of his neighbouring prison cell. The incident has the ring of authenticity about it; Bassani himself spent three months in prison in 1943 for his work with the resistance.

Responding to a telephone call from Alberto, the narrator cycles through the garden by moonlight, across the hardened snow, to find Micòl returned. He kisses her but instantly realizes he has made a mistake. When, shortly afterwards, she becomes ill, he wants to climb the 123 steps to her room, like a prince climbing to his princess in a turret, but is instead persuaded to take the more prosaic lift. If this was that fairytale, he would kiss her now, and they would live happily ever after. It is not a fairytale. She does not respond to his kisses, telling him he is like a brother to her. He realizes he must give up his dream of being with her.

One last time he cycles by the garden's wall, haunted by Ferrara's young lovers cavorting in the shadows. After all those years he summons the courage to climb the wall, even finding a ladder propped up inside. He crosses the garden in a dream. The dark trees, the tennis court, the embankment to the city walls, are all 'clear and definite as if in relief, in a light that was better than daylight', but his own thinking is confused. Noticing the alpine hut they have been using as a changing room, he begins to realize that a mutual friend he has been spending the evenings with, has been visiting Micòl after they part each night. Giampi Malnate does shave very carefully given he is only seeing a friend…

Our narrator pictures her waiting for Malnate in the garden. Of *course*, how could he have been so blind? Perhaps he is right, though Bassani leaves just enough doubt to not fully convince his reader this is any more true than the rest of the tale. In the distance there is a sound, the piazza clock, ringing like Cinderella's chimes at midnight.

The narrator never sees any of them again. We learn that while Alberto died from a wasting disease before the *repubblichini* arrived, the rest of the family was taken, along with much of Ferrara's Jewish population, first to prison, then a concentration camp. He is reflective, even beginning to wonder if he was right about Micòl's 'affair'. After all, she used to say she lived only for today, 'deceptive words that only a real kiss would have stopped her from uttering'. Apparently, that kiss never came.

# Fairytales

## Once Upon a Time...

What is a fairytale without a magical garden? Of all the places in the world, the most captivating are those we learn about at our tiniest. They remain deep within us all as something to aspire towards in the real world.

Fairytale gardens may be part of an enchanted package, such as the one owned by the Beast in *Beauty and the Beast*. *La Belle et la Bête* was published by Gabrielle-Suzanne Barbot de Villeneuve in 1740. Much of the action takes place in the magical grounds of the Beast's castle, where Beauty is imprisoned in her father's place, after he attempted to steal a rose from the Beast's garden.

Sometimes a garden was beautiful once but must be revived through self-sacrifice. In the Polish tale *The Crow*, the youngest of three princesses discovers a ruined castle. Wandering through its shattered garden she finds a wounded crow, which, much like Beauty's beast, is really a cursed prince. By living in silence for two years, then working as a servant for one more, she breaks the spell, restoring the prince, his castle and, most importantly, of course, the garden.

Other former Edens are barriers, such as the overgrown rose garden in *Sleeping Beauty*, which becomes a forest of thorns for the prince to hack his way through in order to bestow a kiss on the slumbering princess. The earliest-known origin story for the tale is in the appropriately named *Perceforest*, an anonymous, Arthurian-style romance from around 1340. The prince in *Rapunzel* fares even worse, when he falls after the witch discovers his love, blinding himself on the thorns growing beneath the tower.

One should, as Beauty's father discovered to his cost, never steal from a fairytale garden. In the Persian folk tale *Leaves of Pearl*, the youngest of three princes, searching for a cure for his father's blindness, breaks into the garden of a beautiful maiden and steals a branch of pearl leaves while she sleeps. Jealous, his brothers throw the lad down a well and take the magical branch to their father, just at the point when the angry maiden teleports the entire garden to the person who stole her leaves. The tale ends happily when the boy crawls out of the well and, unlike his brothers, is able to explain where the leaves came from and why he took them.

Another great Middle Eastern collection has become more famous than most of its component parts. *The One Thousand and One Nights*, comprising mainly medieval folk tales, is from the Islamic Golden Age, around the eighth to the thirteenth century; it first appeared in the English language in the eighteenth. Most gardens in *The One Thousand and One Nights* tend to be of the flowers-made-of-jewels variety, but *The Ruined Man Who Became Rich Again* is a little different.

A once-wealthy Baghdad merchant reduced to labouring in the street, dreams that his fortune lies in Cairo. On arriving, however, he is mistakenly arrested for robbery. The Chief of Police demands to know his story, so the man tells of his dream. The chief laughs – he should take no notice of such fancies. Why, only last night he himself dreamed of a ruined garden in Baghdad which had a mighty fortune buried under the broken fountain! He lets the merchant go. Recognizing the garden and fountain in the police chief's dream as his own, the merchant goes straight home to dig up some treasure.

Not all fairytale gardens are full of such joys. Baba Yaga, of Russian and Slavic folklore, famously lives deep in the forest, in a house on chicken legs, surrounded by a picket fence of bones topped with skulls. Baba Yaga is not always wicked, but another, unnamed witch in *Hansel and Gretel*, from *Grimm's Fairy Tales*, first published in 1812 from much older tales collected by the brothers, is pure evil. Her house, made of cakes and candies, is surrounded by a garden of delicious sugar flowers, all designed to lure children to their deaths. Not all is sweet in Fairytale Land.

# Death's Garden

## *Mort*
## Terry Pratchett, 1987

*'Death's garden was big, neat, and well-tended. It was also very, very black'*

Sir Terry Pratchett's greatest contribution to botanical science is, without doubt, the reannual, a plant that you sow this season to harvest last year. Such wonders of un-nature are found only in Discworld, Pratchett's alternative universe, a giant flat disc supported by four enormous elephants teetering on a giant star turtle.

Mort's father makes wine from reannual grapes, much sought-after by fortune tellers, but his son shows no great aptitude for horticulture, so he takes him to the hiring fair, where he is spotted by Death, who has decided to take on an apprentice.

Always speaking in UPPER CASE, Death is a skeleton, wreathed in black, riding a terrifying pony of the apocalypse and wielding a scythe of luminous thinness. Yet this is satire, both of the real world and of fantasy/ science fiction. Any initial horror at Death's arrival is instantly undercut by a sheet of slippery ice. OH BUGGER. We learn that the horse is called Binky, that Death loves curry and hates people who drown kittens. So did Pratchett, he had a house full of cats.

Death's house is a warren of black and purple, at once sinister and homely. The scythe sits neatly in an umbrella stand, the smell of a fry-up wafts from the kitchen. Mort's new master asks if he wants to learn the uttermost secrets of time and space; when Mort answers in the affirmative,

he is told it is 'DUNG, BOY, DUNG', and directed to the stables to shovel manure for the garden. Later, he will earn his mentor's respect by correctly guessing that there was no philosophical reasoning behind the exercise, just a lot of manure to be shifted.

Death's garden is smart and well-organized, much like something from the human world, but with one major difference. Everything is black – grass, flowers, fruit, trees – and not just dead-black, but shades of black throughout the spectrum of blackness. The garden is tended by the mysterious Albert, who explains that Death made everything, but he's not very imaginative when it comes to colour. He also notes that while the garden is good close-up, the wider vista isn't so well done and the mountains in the distance are positively shoddy. This is a parody of a garden, Albert explains, not the real thing.

Pratchett's garden was reflected in his books – meandering paths, mysterious dead ends, grassy banks and a high walled garden converted from a tennis court

Terry Pratchett knew the real thing. He and his wife Lyn lived an idyllic country life at their Wiltshire home, growing vegetables, fruit, berries and rhubarb. They made plum wine and kept a menagerie of animals including goats, bees, chickens, tortoises and *many* cats. Pratchett's garden was reflected in his books – meandering paths, mysterious dead ends, grassy banks and a high walled garden converted from a tennis court. He famously announced that his idea of a good novel was one that paid enough to buy a greenhouse. Indeed, he used the advances from three books to buy medium-sized glasshouses, quipping that instead of money the publisher should just send him the greenhouse next time. His cover-blurbs often talk about the greenhouses' contents – carnivorous plants – noting that they 'are still doing well' (*Men at Arms*) but 'not as interesting as people believe' (*The Colour of Magic*). He eventually admits, in the fly of *The Last Continent,* that he 'used' to grow carnivorous plants but 'now they've taken over the greenhouse and he avoids going in'. Perhaps this was when he switched to building an observatory in the back garden instead.

Pratchett's universe is not littered with gardens or gardeners, but those he creates are memorable. We learn of Modo, the odd-job dwarf in *Reaper Man* who tends the garden at Unseen University, ex of the

Patrician's Palace, who loves nothing more than his heaving, glowing compost heap. Discworld's scale-challenged answer to Capability Brown, Bloody Stupid Johnson, is a brilliant but flawed Renaissance-man, whose inventions include the ho-ho, a ha-ha that is 50 foot (15 metres) deep, suicidal crazy paving and the one-inch-high (2.5cm) Colossus of Ankh-Morpork. Both Modo and Johnson appear in multiple works.

It is Death's garden, however, that lingers in the imagination. As Mort helps Albert plant out black broccoli, he wonders why his mentor created such a place. Albert suggests it was somewhere 'he could feel at home' but we later learn the truth from Death's daughter Ysabell. Having endured an uncomfortable discussion about not wanting to marry each other, she and Mort take a walk in the garden 'without obligation, of course'. Padding across the black lawn by black lily beds, they call a truce, agreeing not to get married 'for the sake of the children' and turn to deeper matters. They sit on a stone seat beside clipped black hedges, watching shroud-white carp and velvety black water lilies in a pool where a stone lion vomits water from an icy spring. Here, Ysabell reveals that her father made this pastiche of horticultural formality for her. He never visits the garden, he just copied everything from places he has seen on his travels to keep her amused. She stands up for her father as a good wraith; he is fascinated by humanity and is trying *really hard* to act like a human – he even once tried to learn the banjo – he just doesn't always get it right.

Death appears in nearly all of Pratchett's novels. In *Reaper Man* he even becomes temporarily mortal, he is clearly one of the author's favourite characters. He became less enjoyable in 2007 when Pratchett was diagnosed with Alzheimer's disease, but continued to appear in Pratchett's books to the end.

Terry Pratchett finally met his creation in 2015 at the height of his comic powers. He loved gardens and nature, seeing his worlds, both real and imagined, in terms of the earth. He even once likened types of comedy to plants. While he held that 'you can grow wit on a damp flannel', he was adamant: true humour 'needs deep soil'.

# The Garden I Have in Mind

## *My Garden (Book):* Jamaica Kincaid, 1991

*'My garden has no serious intentions, only a series of doubts upon series of doubts'*

Given a hoe, rake, spade, fork and a fat sheaf of seed packets one Mother's Day, Jamaica Kincaid rushed outdoors to sow them all. They never germinated; she had not prepared the soil properly or considered the best place for them, but something else began to sprout in her heart, something that would soon dominate her life.

*My Garden (Book):* is not fiction, but neither is it a traditional memoir. It might be called a miscellany, a notebook, a diary, a collection of musings, a rash of opinions, a smattering of gossip and salty observation, a folio of essays, a manifesto, an *aide-memoire*, but no, it falls under none of those classifications either. Perhaps it is best described as a potpourri of Kincaid's thoughts, fragrant and, on occasion, spicy, combining the joy and honesty of Elizabeth von Arnim (see pages 46–53) with the elegance and frankness of Sei Shōnagon (see pages 64–69). Indeed, its style brings both writers to mind, taking as it does an anecdotal, sometimes list-like format, very loosely following the chronological seasons. Part of its episodic nature may be attributed to its origins in Kincaid's essays and articles for journals and magazines, but this is not just a collection of old features. Care has gone into the order and juxtapositioning of pieces, and it has clearly been reworked for its transition to book form. It is, quite

simply, a gardener's garden book. For who among us has not also bewailed at some point 'what to do?'.

Much like von Arnim's fictional Elizabeth, (the real) Kincaid is forced to learn one of gardening's fundamental principles: the sanctity of patience. She sows a lawn, but is horrified at seeing only small spikes of green appearing the next spring. It takes a neighbour to point out what they are, and that she has inherited something special: a peony garden. She must rethink her plans, creating something new but incorporating what is already there.

A garden, she tells us, is an exercise in memory. Specifically, 'the garden I was making (and am still making and will always be making) resembled a map of the Caribbean and the sea that surrounds it'. Kincaid's current garden is in Vermont, USA, different in almost every respect to the land in which she grew up: Antigua. She does not yet, however, want to talk of such things. We do not know her well enough for intimacies, and for the moment we must stay with safer topics. Plants are a good start. As she begins to understand plants, she has learned that many of her existing evergreens are 'horticulturally undistinguished' yet she feels a fierce loyalty to them. She rails at a visiting botanist who pointed out one particular tree's dullness, who looked only at its scientific inadequacies, seemingly entirely ignorant of a plant's emotional ties. He knew nothing, for example, of the child who measured himself against its trunk, a child who, now grown, she remains in touch with. After another snob told her to grub-out the lot she actively apologized to each

# It is, quite simply, a gardener's garden book

and every tree. The individual concerned will not be invited back.

As she begins to relax, Kincaid slowly invites us, however, into her life. The house she lives in now is at least twenty times the size of the one she grew up in, in a poor country with a tropical climate. She feels uncomfortable about living in a house at all, everything was done outdoors in Antigua. Gardens were yards. Her family had sugar cane, pawpaw, coconut and strange squashes now sold by upmarket American catalogues as 'crookneck'. She detests them, almost as much as she hates the breadfruit all the kids hated, but no, if we do not already know why this should be, we are not yet ready to know.

Much as Elizabeth von Arnim's book spends much time discussing what the author does during the perishingly long winter months, Kincaid is preoccupied with the strangeness of winter. She is particularly ambivalent towards the snow that seems to suffocate the garden. Antigua does not have seasons, indeed she was ten before she encountered cold air, on putting her hand inside a friend's refrigerator. She is suspicious of people who claim to like winter, who find beauty in small things that manage to survive. She is particularly hard on the English garden designer Rosemary Verey, who has actively decided to 'like' winter. Such notions are, Kincaid sniffs, 'just the sort of thing to give pleasure a bad name'.

We may not always agree with such opinions, but we rejoice in her airing them with such delicious candour. Pronounced so openly, so generously, they become intimacies between friends, friends of the kind with whom you may disagree and still enjoy the resulting discussion. We dig-in with her as she arms herself against the Vermont winter, with books and magazines, and 'snippets' from famous gardeners and garden writers such as Christopher Lloyd or Gertrude Jekyll or Graham Stuart Thomas. We rush to the mailbox with her to collect armfuls of catalogues, harrumph with her at the rudeness of the 'puffed-up plantsman's outfit in Connecticut', sigh at the shipment of twigs that was supposed to be fruit trees. We curl up with her on a sofa with the true plantsman's catalogues, the ones with no photographs, or at least the ones with poorly taken photographs snapped with poor-quality cameras. We revel in chatty descriptions of potatoes, we over-order roses and share the triumph of a serendipitous purchase: packets of nasturtium seeds when she meant to buy milk. We puff with her pride at the resulting nasturtium-strewn borders, deflate with her as she realizes Monet's garden got there first.

Just as we are getting comfy, however, Kincaid deftly kicks the rug from our feet. Perhaps it is because we have been so cosy together that the revelation of a friend's mother's casual racism is so shocking, swiftly followed by more, from a man who has come, perhaps fittingly, to rebuild a stone wall.

Still, however, Kincaid does not linger; she re-plunges us into winter. The whole chapter might be a Shōnagon list: 'Suitable Gardening Gifts', even if it is not named as such. A visit to a botanical garden or a museum. Seeds by Thompson & Morgan. Tree peonies. Unusual rhododendrons. A subscription to *Gardens Illustrated*. Membership of the RHS. 'Books are the things I most like to get,' she tells us, impishly recommending stapling together the pages of all introductions and wondering how she can ask for two copies of her favourites: one to keep in pristine condition, one to get grubby around the roses. She both loves and hates 'the authoritative and the overbearing' voices of the great gardeners, the kind that bully her in the first sentence, sometimes, even, in the title. She has a similarly refreshing ambivalence to some of horticulture's sacred cows, harbouring an antipathy, for example, towards Sissinghurst and its creators: Vita Sackville-West and Harold Nicolson. In a *tour-de force* comparison with Nina Simone's autobiography, she talks of a life so dramatic it can hardly be dramatized, as opposed to lives so empty they fall back on petty dramas. 'The world cannot be left out of the garden,' she observes.

We are deep into Kincaid's world now, *now* we may learn something of her childhood. We learn how her mother left her with another woman who in turn left her alone to have sex with a strange man. Young Jamaica lost herself in the bright crimsons and purples of the portulaca in the strange man's garden, pretending she was from somewhere else. She calls the plant 'bachelors' button' and later, while discussing names, notes that 'to name is to possess'. Talking of the conqueror and the conquered, via gardens such as Painshill in Surrey, England, visited by gardener and slave-owner Thomas Jefferson, she is clear about the relationship between conquest and gardening. As one from the conquered class, living in a conquered place, she did not know the names of the plants from the place she is from. Antigua's botanical garden displayed plants of the British Empire. What was there before the hated breadfruit, sent to the West Indies by that great plant 'appropriator' Joseph Banks as cheap food for slaves? She is surprised to see cotton plants in flower, she only ever saw cotton before as something to be picked.

Kincaid, too, becomes a 'plant hunter', travelling on an organized trip to China to collect seeds. She visits famous gardens around the world for inspiration and great horticultural events to celebrate gardening's cutting-edge. The Chelsea Flower Show is like 'a giant birthday party'.

We move, Shōnagon-like, through episodic chapters consisting only of a fruit tree order or a letter sent to a nurseryman. For spring is beginning. Suddenly everything is coming at once. Like von Arnim, Kincaid is desperate to get back out into the garden after examining all those others with a critical but curious eye. 'We who covet our neighbour's garden must finally return to our own,' she tells us, admitting that some things in life can never completely satisfy us. 'I shall never have the garden I have in mind, but that for me is the joy of it'.

# Somewhere in West Kensington

## 'The Door in the Wall'
H.G. Wells, 1906

*'In the instant of coming into it one was exquisitely glad – as only in rare moments and when one is young and joyful'*

Despite an early training in biology, Herbert George Wells is best known as a futurist, for looking to a world with robots and time machines, rather than indulging in bucolic memories of paradise gardens. If he talks about plants at all, they are evil red weeds or vampiric orchids, which is why the short story 'The Door in the Wall' is unusual in describing a lost Eden with a tenderness that renders the reader edgy with suspicion throughout. Romance in a Wells novel? That can never end well…

Indeed, we learn very early on in this tale of loss and missed opportunities that the bearer of such memories is now dead. Our narrator Redmond is himself unsure about the story his friend Lionel Wallace has told him. Is this man, an up-and-coming politician, 'the possessor of an inestimable privilege' or 'the victim or a fantastic dream'?

Redmond is keen to make one thing clear: his friend was brilliant, surpassing him in intelligence and attainment at school and continuing to a glittering career that would have seen him in the Cabinet had he lived.

Wallace is taking a chance relating his story to Redmond. Revelation has never served him well in the past. Yet by the time he takes Redmond into his confidence obsession has grown into something he cannot contain.

'I am haunted,' he says, as *fin-de-siècle* rationalism battles with experiences he has known since the age of five.

Wallace recounts the first time he encountered the door in the wall. A lonely child, his mother dead and his father coldly authoritarian, he walks us through a dull, grey street, somewhere in West Kensington, London, in autumn. Its dirty shops, cabs and street traders are forgotten, however, when he catches sight of a white wall covered in a curtain of scarlet Virginia creeper. Horse chestnut leaves litter the ground but Wallace's child's eye spots a green door. His sixth sense tells him he should not turn the handle, but the foreboding is vanquished by an overwhelming desire to do exactly that. By now we, too, are desperate to know what is behind the door, but Wells has carefully primed us. We dread whatever will be there.

We are nonplussed when, instead of monsters, mad scientists and warped experiments, we are confronted by a magical garden. Wallace is exhilarated, overcome with joy, but we still do not quite believe his luck, especially when two panthers appear. All they do is play with a ball.

Wells's description of the garden does not read like a horticulturist's dream. His 'perfectly clean' marble-edged flower borders, seem to be at odds with the 'weedless' beds 'rich with untended flowers', but he is not describing a real garden here. His is a luminous fairyland. The spikes of delphiniums, marble seats, doves, shady trees and flower-strewn sundial are as real as the capuchin monkey, fountains, kindly girl and new playmates. Wallace's giddy abandonment as he tells us 'Heaven knows where West Kensington had suddenly got to', is palpable.

While the garden behind the wall is clearly not real, Wells must have found inspiration somewhere. Perhaps it was the gardens at Uppark country house, where his mother worked as a housekeeper and young Herbert visited. Perhaps, though, his strange paradise is a conglomeration of illustrations in the many books the twelve-year-old Wells read while recovering from a broken leg in 1874.

Wherever the inspiration came from, 'It was like I was coming home', Wallace tells us. Alas, on returning to his actual home, he is beaten by his father for telling lies and further punished by his aunt for 'wicked persistence'. Worst of all, his fairytale books are taken away from him.

From now on the garden will evade him or, to be more precise, he will evade the garden. It is not always available to him and does not appear in the same place every time, but it does reappear. He chooses not to re-enter it. The first time he needs to get to school, and intends to return later. He makes the mistake of telling the school gossip and, on being hounded by bullies, tries to prove his story by finding the door in their company. It is, of course, nowhere to be found. Other children make his life difficult but when he cries at night it is not because of them, but for his lost world.

Over the years Wallace is given ample opportunity to re-enter his dream, but each time he provides himself with a perfectly rational excuse not to. He glimpses it on his way to Oxford for a scholarship, stops the cabman, then changes his mind. Was this a missed opportunity? Or would his chasing this rainbow have cost him his scholarship in the real world? The next time he spots the door it is at Earl's Court, three steps out of his way at most, but he is on his way to a date and passes it by. Another time he is rushing to the House of Commons for a division on a much-needed parliamentary vote, on a later occasion the door appears on his way to visit his dying father. Most recently, his excuse is even thinner – he was passing by with someone who could promote him and didn't want to look strange.

Wallace's life has been one of choices – choices for a better life, perhaps at the expense of what might have been. He is constantly haunted by what people might think – even now, ten weeks since his last opportunity to enter the garden and full of 'inappeasable regrets', he worries what people will think of him grieving for – and sometimes near-audibly lamenting – a garden?

The last time we see Wallace alive he has made a decision. The next time he sees the door, he will go through it.

'The Door in the Wall' was first published in the *Daily Chronicle* in 1906. It was subsequently published in *The Country of the Blind and Other Stories* in 1911. There have been many interpretations, from Bernard Bergonzi's suggestion that the garden is a womb, to W. Warren Wager's assertion that the story is a warning not to be seduced by unreason. The sheer number of question marks in its final paragraph suggest that even Wells was not entirely sure what really happened to Lionel Wallace. Should we feel sorry for him? After all, his choices led to a life of material success. Yet an overwhelming sense of melancholy envelopes us in the final lines as we discover that he did, indeed, finally locate his – or perhaps 'a' – lost door.

# The Monkey Garden

## *The House on Mango Street*
Sandra Cisneros, 1984

*'We took over the garden we had been afraid to go into'*

Most of Esperanza's earliest memories involve her family constantly moving, from rental property to rental property. The house on Mango Street is not the home of her dreams, the one she imagined when Papa used to buy his lottery ticket: a big white house with trees and grass in a great big garden with no fence. Reality is less romantic. They had to get out of their last place fast, thanks to a burst water pipe.

The house on Mango Street is small and red with sharp, tight steps. Instead of Esperanza's fantasy front yard, four meagre elm trees planted by the city struggle by the kerb. At the back there's a small garage for the car they don't have and a tiny garden that looks even smaller in contrast with the buildings around it.

No, it's not the family's dream home, but it is theirs. They don't have to pay rent or keep the noise down or share the garden with the people upstairs. Her mother tells her it's just for the time being. Papa agrees – temporary, he insists. But while Esperanza is young, she's already old in some matters. 'I know how these things go,' she admits.

Sandra Cisneros's first novel *The House on Mango Street* is a coming-of-age tale set in one of the poorer, mainly Puerto Rican, suburbs of Chicago. The book clearly draws from Cisneros's own experience of growing up in a family constantly moving between Mexico and the USA. Profoundly aware of her surroundings and inequality and being the 'one daughter' in her father's 'six sons and one daughter' – she began her writer's habit of collecting the stories of people very young, observing the characters around her in Humboldt Park on Chicago's west side. She has been committed ever since to telling the stories of marginalized people, especially women.

*The House on Mango Street* takes an episodic, thematic approach, and it is not always chronologically linear. Instead, we are introduced to people, ideas and incidents that invite us into a world that outsiders might find baffling. People here are rarely all good or all bad, each has to find their way through difficult lives. 'You can never have too much sky,' Esperanza tells us, 'Here there is too much sadness and not enough sky'. She talks of dusty geraniums and window boxes with cockroaches while dreaming of butterflies and flowers and beautiful things. 'We take what we can get and make the best of it'.

Mango Street is a poor neighbourhood, but seen through Ezperanza's eyes, it is nevertheless a functioning community. Gangsters are people's relatives; they might give kids a ride in their fancy car before, minutes later, a police chase wrecks the vehicle. The children are street-smart through experience. They learn who and what to avoid. The Rose Vargas kids, for example, are bad, though Esperanza admits they can't help it – there are too many of them for one mother to control. They bend trees and bounce between cars 'without respect for all things living, including themselves'. When another neighbour moves out and all the kids move into her old garden – mostly dirt and a pile of boards that used to be a garage – the children hold The First Annual Tarzan Jumping Contest in a tree 'with fat arms and mighty families of squirrels in the higher branches'. The winning child breaks both his arms.

While some of the girls seem to be enjoying the growing attention of men. Esperanza does not and she feels left behind. She identifies with the skinny necks and pointy elbows of the struggling elms outside the front of her house. They are 'the only ones who understand me and I am the only one who understands them'. Like her, these 'four, raggedy excuses' don't belong here. She knows – and, we realize, shares – their secret strength:

their roots, ferocious and deep. 'They bite the sky with violent teeth,' she tells us, and 'never quit their anger'. When she is at a low ebb, she clings onto the image of those trees, which reach and never forget to reach.

Esperanza is in her own 'quiet war', trying to find her identity. She leaves the family dinner table 'like a man', without replacing the chair or picking up her plate.

By the time the monkey garden appears, the reader might be forgiven for thinking that Esperanza is a young woman – perhaps 18 or 20. It comes as a shock to realize that she and her girlfriends are not even yet in the eighth grade – in American schools, around 13 or 14. She may be as young as 12 years old. While the garden is local, Esperanza appears never to have entered it in its heyday, thanks to the horrific screeching of the owners' caged monkey, a terrifying but ultimately pitiful creature.

The monkey doesn't live there anymore. He moved to Kentucky and 'took his people with him'. Esperanza is glad; she hated hearing his screams. Slowly, the local kids venture into the abandoned yard. This latter-day Garden of Eden, with 'green apples as hard as knees' will gradually become corrupted by humans, resulting in a disturbing loss of innocence.

The monkey garden was once well kept, with sunflowers 'as big as flowers on Mars' – Esperanza literally dreams of outer space – and 'dizzy bees', 'bow-tied fruit flies' and 'sweet, sweet peach trees', but it begins to disintegrate even as the children start to play there. Colourful spiders and beetles scuttle through weeds Esperanza likens to 'squinty-eyed stars'. Someone starts a rumour that the monkey garden has been there since the beginning of time. Stories swirl of the bones of murdered buccaneers; of a piece of coal that was, or so the kids whisper, once the eye of a unicorn. Everything is dreamy, filled with the 'sleepy smell of rotting wood'. One child, Eddie Vargas, actually falls into a Rip Van Winkle-like slumber, under a hibiscus bush.

Slowly, this horticultural sleeping beauty descends into jungle, though we are never given any indication of how long this is all taking. Months? Years? Centuries? This warped fairytale remains shadowy. Plants grow out of control. Dead cars pop up 'like mushrooms' and the place changes from being a childhood haven to somewhere altogether more dangerous.

Esperanza eventually admits she wanted to die in the monkey garden, then reveals that, in despair, she tried to fulfil the wish one day.

The garden becomes the scene for a particularly painful episode, when Esperanza tries to protect her friend Sally whom she believes is being intimidated by a group of boys. Missing the signs that Sally is, in reality, taunting the lads, egging them on, Esperanza arms herself with sticks and a brick, but is just told by Sally to go home. The kids laugh at her; a big boy takes Sally away. We share Esperanza's sense of foreboding, not least because we have more of an idea what will happen to Sally than does the innocent Esperanza.

Suddenly the garden where she has enjoyed playing so much is sullied. Her friend has shamed her, left her behind, betrayed her. We later learn that another boy grabbed Esperanza in the monkey garden, covering her with 'sour' kisses. We do not learn the details, but suspect the worst: rape, right there, in her erstwhile paradise.

Esperanza is desperate with shame. She wants to hide herself in the garden's undergrowth, wills herself to stop breathing, 'but not even the monkey garden would have me'. It is the last day she ever goes there.

There is no going back. Sally marries a marshmallow salesman 'in a state where it's legal to get married before the eighth grade'. True to her name, however, Esperanza – 'Hope' – wants more. She has been damaged but she is not broken. She is going to have her own house, with pretty purple petunias. She is going to get out, armed with her books and paper, and she is going to tell the hidden stories of Mango Street. The monkey garden – and what happened there – is part of her life, but it will never define her.

# Wilsthorpe

## 'Mr Humphreys and His Inheritance'
M.R. James, 1911

*'The dankness and darkness, and smell of crushed goosegrass and nettles were anything but cheerful'*

Unexpected bequests from previously unheard-of relatives never end well in an M.R. James story. Yet young Mr Humphreys persists, trying to find 'normal' explanations for the mounting terror he feels on visiting the estate that he has recently inherited.

Montague Rhodes James is not one of literature's famous gardeners. Far happier in an ancient church or surrounded by obscure medieval tomes in his rooms at Kings College, Cambridge, the closest he is likely to have ventured into the great outdoors would have been the college's immaculately kept Back Lawn, the tranquillity of the Fellows' Garden or the Arts and Crafts intimacy of the Provost's Garden. James was Provost (head of the college) for 13 years before becoming Vice-Chancellor, but there is little evidence that he was particularly moved by the university's formal gardens. When, in 'Mr Humphreys and His Inheritance', the bailiff's wife babbles to the newly arrived Wilsthorpe legatee that he has arrived too late in the season for the 'better' garden parties, Mr Humphreys expresses his disappointment with 'a gleam of relief'. James may have enjoyed gardens more when he arrived at Eton in 1918, where his great friend, classics master Henry Elford Luxmoore, had built an extraordinary 'island garden' in the Thames from the remains of an underwater waste site. It seems unlikely, however, that James was inspired to take up the trowel himself.

It might be argued that this apparent indifference led to some of the creepiest images from his works being set in the alien surroundings of a garden: the haunting figure that crawls across the lawn in 'The Mezzotint', for example, or the sinister branches knocking against Sir Richard Fell's bedroom window in 'The Ash-tree'; the horrifying face staring at Mrs Anstruther from a box tree after she has had an ancient stake removed from a shrubbery to make room for her 'Rose Garden'. Then again, James found potential for horror in everything, and gardens were fair game, alongside bedsheets, binoculars, scrapbooks and whistles.

Mr Humphreys's garden at Wilsthorpe (an entirely invented location) is essentially a device for James's latest 'antiquarian story'; a vehicle through which he can explore his first love: history. A more horticulturally minded writer might feel uncomfortable about a hedge maze that after 40 years of neglect still looks like one. James has no such qualms about using artistic licence.

Wilsthorpe's only remaining staff member, the head gardener, is not available as we first experience the estate. Humphreys and his bailiff Cooper are left to explore the grounds alone. James has little to say about the garden save that has been kept well and the stock is excellent. Only when the pair find their way to the ancient-looking Temple of Friendship, however, is James the architectural historian at last on solid ground. The tempo changes as we learn that it is constructed of imported Italian marble and based on the Sybil's Temple at Tivoli, Rome, that the date is '1770 or thereabouts' and that it is 'a pleasant favour of the Grand Tour'. Humphreys discovers some strange, circular stones inside, with letters carved into them. Mr Cooper suggests they have perhaps been removed from a mysterious hedge maze below the temple. Locked for decades, it is hidden behind a high brick wall, though no one knows why. There is some competition among the locals as to who will get inside first. Lady Wardrop, who is writing a book about mazes, was rebuffed without reason when she applied for access some time ago.

While Cooper goes to find the key, Humphreys tests the nettle-clogged gates with his boot. To his surprise, the rusted iron padlock crumbles. The yew, untouched for decades, is overgrown but not impassable. As he hacks through the 'dankness and darkness', Humphreys feels uneasy. A strange, stone column at the centre, topped by a copper ball engraved with figures, is almost entirely choked by undergrowth. Humphreys takes it for a celestial globe. He cannot see the outlines, but vows to return the next day once the gardeners have cleared the pathways.

That evening, in a typically Jamesian 'library' scene, Humphreys reads an account of a young man who enters a labyrinth 'like Theseus in the Attick Tale', in search of a great jewel. He is found in a death-like swoon, babbling of monsters. Humphreys suspects his uncle locked his own labyrinth after reading the horrific tale. The next morning he shows the maze to Mr Cooper's daughter, who is 'on the tentacles of expectation'. Despite the area having been tidied by the gardeners, the centre now eludes them.

Humphreys is thwarted in other ways, too. His sketches are ruined by the rain. A telegram from town calls him away. When he and Cooper finally rediscover the centre the copper ball is carved not with astrological figures but horrific inversions of the constellations, '... an assemblage of the patriarchs of evil'. The globe is uncomfortably hot to Cooper's touch, though Humphreys cannot feel the heat. Finally allowed access, Lady Wardrop believes that they are being watched. Again, Humphreys experiences nothing.

Instead, he is haunted by horticulture. By moonlight, he notices a small, thin Irish yew, weirdly out of place in the garden below. The following night a dark lump of growth, 'dank and unhealthy', threatens to obscure the downstairs windows. Humphreys only begins to understand true horror, however, when his own space – his beloved library – is invaded, firstly by bats, then terrible visions.

'Mr Humphreys and His Inheritance' is one of James's more confusing tales. Included as a makeweight 'to fill up the volume' in *More Ghost Stories of an Antiquary*, it does not carry the cosy feel of his Christmas chillers, neither are its ends as neatly tied as many of his stories. Even so, the reader is unsurprised when, after the story's sinister denouement, the labyrinth is grubbed up, an act even the maze-obsessed Lady Wardrop cannot condemn. Humphreys himself, however, cannot quite forgive his uncle for destroying the old papers relating to the maze, revealing, perhaps, James's own priorities regarding gardens and documents.

# The World Tree

'The best and greatest of all trees;
its branches spread over all the world,
and reach up above heaven'

*Prose Edda,* Snorri Sturluson, *c.*1220

Just seven manuscripts remain of Snorri Sturluson's *Prose Edda,* composed in Iceland around 1220, none of them complete. Even so, the work remains our best source for the Norse folklore of Scandinavia. Much would be familiar to Sturluson's contemporary audience, but to modern eyes the Norse world is strange and dark. At its centre, however, lies something found in cultures across the globe: an imaginary axis between the world's celestial poles where the earth meets the heavens, the *axis mundi.* This most commonly takes the form of a great tree.

The world tree usually has three specific areas: the gods live in the highest branches, while the trunk is the world of humans. Deep in the earth, the tree's roots are the domain of the lords of the underworld.

Yggdrasil is one of literature's most famous examples, the great ash that makes up the Norse universe, also described in the anonymous *Poetic Edda.* A great eagle lives in its topmost branches surveying the world's comings and goings. He has never met Niðhöggr the Dragon, which gnaws at Yggdrasil's roots in the underworld. The Norns, three goddesses representing the past, present and future, spin the world's fate in the tree's shade, while Jörmungandr the serpent wraps itself around the nine worlds nestled in its branches.

While at first sight dissimilar to Yggrdrasil, the Garden of Eden's Tree of Knowledge in the Christian Bible also has a snake lurking in its boughs. Like many creatures in such stories, the snake represents evil and, even worse, the knowledge of evil. In Siberian shamanism the world tree's roots are also home to lizards and frogs. One of the greatest epics of early world literature, the Sumerian *Epic of Gilgamesh* tells how Gilgamesh kills the dark, ghostly serpent of the goddess Inanna's Huluppu Tree, allowing the other creatures to escape.

If there is a bird in a world tree, it will be wise, all-knowing and generally good. The Siberian world tree's birds roost alongside the Sun and the Moon. In Persian mythology, the Haoma Tree, responsible for the seeds of all the world's plants, is home to the Simurgh, an enormous, benevolent bird.

The Huluppu and Haoma are mythical plants but other world trees are enormous versions of real species. The Mayan people venerated a giant kapok, while the ancient Egyptians gave their gods a mighty sycamore. For Mongolic and Turkic peoples, the tree is a birch or beech. The most popular world tree is an oak. In Lithuania and Finland it grows normally, if all the way up to the heavens, but in some Baltic and Slavic traditions the tree is presented upside down, with its roots in the skies, while its branches sweep the Earth. The Chinese Fusang or Spirit Tree, described in the ancient text *The Classic of Mountains and Seas*, is said to be a great mulberry or sometimes a hibiscus, inhabited by a roost of celestial chickens that awaken the globe's poultry each morning with their crowing. According to Chinese mythology, ten ravens live in the tree, one of which leaves home each day to carry the Sun across the sky.

Whichever culture the world tree appears in, it is nearly always also considered the Tree of Life. In Haiti it represents the way all life interconnects, though a story told by the Wapangwa people of Tanzania explains how this may be interpreted in different ways. According to legend, the animals of the world saw the tree as a source of sustenance for life, a gift, to be eaten and enjoyed. The humans wanted to keep it pure, to worship it without touching its leaves or fruit. In the battle that ensued, the humans dominated, but they lost the goodwill of the animals and now the two can no longer communicate via spoken language.

No more starkly drawn than in 2001's *American Gods* where Neil Gaiman has transported Yggdrasil to a farm in Virginia, USA, today the world tree remains as potent a symbol in literature as ever.

# Cornelius van Baerle's Garden

## *The Black Tulip*
Alexandre Dumas, 1850

*'Van Baerle had gained the affections of his fellow citizens by completely shunning the pursuit of politics, absorbed as he was in the peaceful pursuit of cultivating tulips'*

When a hero is described on his first appearance in a story as 'a truly happy mortal' we know instinctively that, within a couple of pages, his paradise will begin to fall apart.

Even paradise is in short supply as Dumas *père*'s Netherlands-set adventure opens, however. It is 1672. Cornelius and Johan de Witt have been – and indeed were, for they are real historical figures – falsely accused of treason. In the novel, the gaoler's daughter, Rosa, helps the brothers escape but they are recaptured and their (real) violent, messy death courtesy of 'King Mob', leaves the reader gasping.

There are letters that would prove their innocence, or at least there *were* letters. Cornelius de Witt entrusted the bundle to his (fictional) godson, 'honest' Cornelius van Baerle, 'who knows so much, yet thinks of nothing but flowers'. 'It will be his ruin,' predicts Johan. Yet van Baerle has followed his godfather's instructions and preserved the bundle unopened in a drawer. Only the reader knows he was watched as he did so.

Van Baerle is unbothered by politics. He is consumed by that other seventeenth-century Dutch obsession: tulips. The 1670s are a little late for the true 'Tulip Mania', the historical financial bubble blown then burst in the 1630s, but tulip fancying remained hugely popular and rarities still fetched tremendous prices. Even in the grips of mania, however, no one thought of growing anything as impossible as a black tulip. The 100,000-guilder prize offered by the Horticultural Society of Haarlem for the first person to breed a truly black tulip was invented by Dumas in this novel in 1850, but it instantly gripped the public imagination.

Cornelius van Baerle's mansion in Dort (now Dordrecht), then, is a welcome contrast to the horrors of The Hague. Advised by his father to eat, drink and spend his money, and not to go into politics like his godfather, van Baerle has studied plants and insects, then collected and classified the flora of the Dutch islands before becoming enamoured of tulips. Thanks to hard work and study, his garden is now sought by horticulturists 'as the galleries and libraries of Alexandria were visited by illustrious Roman travellers'.

Thanks to hard work and study, his garden is now sought by horticulturists 'as the galleries and libraries of Alexandria were visited by illustrious Roman travellers'

Mynheer van Baerle's tulips, his beds, borders, pots, pits, drying rooms and bulb-drawers are the talk of Holland. He has named his three new varieties for his mother, father and godfather and gained the people's affection in his 'peaceful pursuits'. One thing in which he does not excel, however, is in his powers of observation. He has not noticed his neighbour, who is rather less enamoured with van Baerle than the rest of the country.

Isaac Boxtel has been a tulip-fancier much longer than the young upstart. Less wealthy than his neighbour, he has had to work hard for his blooms. He knows the temperature of his cold frames 'to a twentieth part of a degree' and the strength of the currents of air in his garden, and can temper both to his will. He has achieved modest success for his pains.

We first see van Baerle's garden through Boxtel's jealous eyes, a couple of years before the opening chapters. He has climbed a ladder to look over his neighbour's wall to see gardens perfectly laid out, of loam mixed with river mud, surrounded by a border of turf for easy tending. Every provision has been made, from sufficient shade against the noonday sun to a swanky new building for nurturing young plants. Boxtel had had to give up his bedroom to nurture *his* plantlets.

Consumed with jealousy, Boxtel begins to spy on the oblivious van Baerle weeding, manuring, watering and cosseting his charges. Boxtel starts to neglect his own plants. His bulbs rot, his seedlings dry up, his tulips wither. His name disappears from the list of notable growers but all he can think of is his neighbour's successes. He considers sabotage but even to his diseased mind, killing a tulip is a horrible crime. Eventually, he cannot help himself. He ties two cats together and throws them over the wall, trembling with excitement – or perhaps horror – at the mess they make of van Baerle's garden.

When Cornelius de Witt gives the mysterious bundle to his godson, Boxtel the fanatic automatically assumes it contains tulips. As his neighbour puts it away unopened, however, he realizes that no true fancier could not open a parcel of bulbs. It must be political papers.

A writer of swashbucklers, rather than a gardener, Alexandre Dumas knew that obsession always engenders conflict. He moved the Tulip Mania craze forward a few decades to coincide with the political intrigues in the court of William, Prince of Orange because tulips make excellent devices to drive a plot. He does not seem to have been moved enough to describe the flowers' intrinsic beauty, however.

We return to August 1672, and van Baerle is close to producing his black tulip. He will give the 100,000 guilders to the poor, as he is ultimately more interested in his true prize – the scientific name he will give his baby: *Tulipa nigra* 'Barlaeensis'.

A messenger arrives with de Witt's instruction to destroy the letters but van Baerle fails to read it before he is arrested by the guards secretly alerted by Boxtel. Even now he could escape by jumping out of a window, but this would destroy his tulips, and he just can't do it.

Boxtel sneaks into van Baerle's garden in search of the tulip bulb and dreaming of the Latin name it will bear: *Tulipa nigra Boxtellensis*. In vain, he digs up the van Baerle garden: van Baerle has divided his precious bulb into three 'suckers' and taken them with him.

In the same prison cell once occupied by his godfather, van Baerle encounters the brutal gaoler Gryphus and Rosa, his beautiful daughter.

It might be argued that Rosa is the true hero of this book. Her constant resourcefulness and use of slight opportunities keep hope alive. Her help is not always appreciated. Van Baerle rejects her offer to help him escape: he will tell the truth at his trial. His honesty does him no good. 'About to be murdered for having thought too much of tulips,' he gives Rosa his precious bulbs, telling her to send to his garden for soil 'from border number six'. She should call the resulting flower *Tulipa nigra rosa Barlaeensis*, win the prize and marry a good man that she loves.

In one of several barely believable coincidences, van Baerle is saved at the last minute by the arrival of William, Prince of Orange, who commutes his sentence to life imprisonment.

Loevestein is a real castle near Dort which, in the seventeenth century, was used as a prison. Incarcerated there, van Baerle dreams of his garden – and the woman he loves. Rosa is more practical, arranging the transferral of her father – and herself – to Loevestein. She returns van Baerle's bulbs – and, secretly, his love. For safety he takes one 'sucker'; she keeps the other two. He instructs her on how to grow them secretly in the prison garden but suggests she check for rats, both of the rodent and human varieties.

Dumas spends much time over the growing love of van Baerle and Rosa, and the barriers to their shared happiness. Gryphus grinds the first of the precious bulbs underfoot to the horror of not only van Baerle, but a mysterious stranger who has arrived pretending to court the gaoler's daughter. Rosa outwits both her father and 'Jacob' (a poorly disguised Boxtel) but she also keeps van Baerle guessing, as a punishment for seemingly loving his tulip more than her. Ultimately, she realizes the only way she can stop the bulb being her rival is to be its mother.

The flower blooms and the story picks up pace, with much dashing around in carriages, bolting through the night on horseback and fantasies on the part of various characters as to the tulip's eventual scientific name.

## He has one small hope left, that the carriage may pass his old house and that he might catch a glimpse of his garden

By now Boxtel is so addled he no longer thinks of himself as a thief; he has dedicated his life to this bulb, he deserves it. Van Baerle, who has been caught defending himself against Gryphus, is being moved, presumably to his death, to The Hague. He has one small hope left, that the carriage may pass his old house and that he might catch a glimpse of his garden. He wonders if his borders have been spoiled.

In Haarlem, it is the Feast of the Tulip and there is much confusion. The Horticultural Society, dressed 'gay as a meadow', finally have their black tulip, brought forth on a litter of white velvet, trimmed in gold, but who grew it? The beautiful woman standing with the bulb like 'two orphan sisters' or the well-known tulip-fancier Isaac Boxtel? It will take a *deus ex machina* to announce the winner, in Latin, of course…

*The Black Tulip* was an invention entirely from Dumas's mind, but it caught a nerve in nineteenth-century society. The search for a black blooming variety has continued ever since, and there are some very dark varieties, but even today, none is truly black.

# The Garden of Monsieur T—

## *No Tomorrow*
## Vivant Denon, 1777

*'Through the transparent crepe of a beautiful summer night, our imagination made an island that was in front of our pavilion an enchanted place'*

The anonymous narrator of Vivant Denon's Sahara-dry, erotic comedy of manners is clear from the start: he was an innocent. Not sexually, of course, it seems no one was in eighteenth-century high society. Everyone was having an affair with someone. At the beginning of *No Tomorrow*, our narrator has been dismissed by his more experienced lover, before, to his great delight, taken back. It is with surprise, then, that, while alone at the theatre, he finds himself invited into his mistress's friend's box.

Things move very quickly. Almost immediately Madame T— (the mistress's friend) sends a servant to her guest's house to tell the staff he will not be returning that night. Opera forgotten, they leave; her carriage is outside Paris before he knows what's happening. He is confused. Madame T— is married and he knows she's in the middle of an affair; what does she want with him? They change horses, then again, as a mysterious moon illuminates a 'pure' sky with its 'voluptuous' half-light.

Monsieur T—'s chateau is brightly lit. Everything inside is joyful except, perhaps unsurprisingly, Monsieur T— himself, at the sight of his wife with a young man. Yet the unwanted husband melts into the background and Madame T— takes her bewildered young conquest outside onto the terrace.

The night is superb. The moon's 'veil' allows 'free reign to the imagination'; flesh glimpsed *déshabillé* is so much more exciting than vulgar nudity. Capricious and teasing, Madame T— leads him to a grassy bank. Between the thickly planted trees our narrator catches flashes of undulating greenery sweeping down towards the Seine. The garden too, is flirting with him.

*No Tomorrow* reads like the literary equivalent of a Fragonard painting; a confection of coquettes on swings, swooning paramours and mysterious gardens filled with blousy, overblown trees and statues of conspiratorial putti, fingers firmly on lips. There were hundreds of such 'Enlightenment' landscapes across Europe, harking back to Classical ideals while acknowledging the clash between the Age of Reason and the crumbling remains of real ancient Greek and Roman cities being discovered by Europe's Grand Tourists. At once formal and artfully 'overgrown', filled with grottos and temples, they might have been – and, indeed, sometimes were – built for clandestine rendezvous. Denon's garden might be any of scores of Northern French gardens such as the Moulin Joly, the Désert de Retz or even the Jardin de la Reine at Versailles.

'Kisses are like confidences,' confides our narrator, 'they attract each other'. Faux-alarmed at the passions the garden seems to be arousing in them, the couple feign a desire to return to safety indoors.

'In the midst of metaphysical discussions', however, they turn back down 'the great path of sentiment' to the garden. Madame T— points to a pavilion, that has, in the past, 'witnessed the sweetest of moments'. What a pity she doesn't have the key. But oh, what a surprise – it's been left open! Love's sanctuary 'took possession of us', he admits, 'our knees buckled'.

While *No Tomorrow* is an erotic tale, it is far too elegant to be pornographic. Love here is real, just fleeting. Nature fills the couple. The air is cooler. The river ripples in the distance. 'Let us leave this dangerous place,' whispers Madame T— of a garden that was only recently a haven. She cannot help constantly looking behind her as they return to the house.

Inside, the garden lingers in a rose he has plucked for his lover's hair, but she has more wonders for him. In what he describes as 'an initiation ceremony' she takes him to a temple-like mirrored chamber. It is a fantasy of the garden outside with arbours, porticoes, flowers and grottos. Just as he marvels at an 'artistically painted' birds' view of a grove of trees, with statues and carpet imitating grass, a cleverly contrived mechanism sends the couple onto their backs and into a mound of cushions.

Madame T— asks if her young swain can ever love his countess as much as he loves her, but before he can answer the moment is broken by the hurried arrival of a confidante. It is morning; the entire chateau is awake. Our hero finds himself in an anonymous corridor with no idea where his bedchamber is. He stumbles back out into the garden, but there is no longer comfort there, only Madame T—'s official lover. From now on, his awakening will become ruder with every passing minute.

Denon's French title, *Point de Lendemain*, literally translates as 'No Tomorrow', and his characters often appear to live only for the moment. Similarly hedonistic values appear in Choderlos de Laclos's *Les Liaisons Dangereuses* published five years later. The liaisons in both are almost theatrical. They have little to do with love, everything to do with romance. Seduction is a game and, in *No Tomorrow* especially, the garden plays the role of an enabler.

Alas, for the French nobility 'tomorrow' did come, in the form of the French Revolution. Denon managed to slip past the guillotine but the people he writes about with such joie de vivre would have ended up under its blade had they really existed.

Denon would reinvent himself in the new French Empire, even joining Napoleon Bonaparte's Egyptian campaign. A son of the Enlightenment, he made sketches of monuments, buildings and cities and wrote a travelogue of his experiences. On his return, he was put in charge of Napoleon's looted treasure at the Louvre. His erotic literary excursion now lived a separate life, constantly reprinted, but now attributed to Claude-Joseph Dorat. A pornographic version, *La Nuit Merveilleuse,* was published anonymously. *No Tomorrow* would retain an underground popularity but those hedonistic days before the revolution were gone, leaving only the faintest whiff of a distant perfumed garden.

As she takes leave of her baffled young lover, Madame T— admits 'I owe you many pleasures', then immediately continues 'but I have paid you with a beautiful dream'. The same, perfumed dream still lingers today, albeit faintly.

# 3765, Alta Brea Crescent, West Hollywood

## *The Big Sleep*
## Raymond Chandler, 1939

*'"Somebody built a filling station on my jaw." "What did you expect, Mr Marlowe – orchids?"'*

Philip Marlowe is wearing his powder blue suit and black wool clocked socks. He is neat, clean, shaved – and sober. He has to be, the only plant currently suitable for his dusty downtown office is tumbleweed and his prospective client has four million dollars. Hollywood, Los Angeles, is famous for its sunshine and palm trees. By contrast, Raymond Chandler's benighted LA streets are permanently polished by torrential rain. They cower under bolts of lightning, lurk behind billows of beach fog. The only green we might expect in his brand of hard-boiled detective fiction is in ever-changing traffic lights and flashing neon signs. So when Chandler mentions plants and gardens, it's worth taking notice.

General Sternwood's butler has Marlowe wait in the lobby. Gazing out of the French window, he spies 'a wide sweep of emerald grass' and ornamental trees 'trimmed as carefully as poodle dogs'. The maroon Packard convertible seems almost unnecessary in describing the Sternwood family; we already had their mettle with the poodles.

Marlowe's first encounter with a Sternwood, the younger daughter, a girl of dangerous cuteness 'with sharp predatory teeth', is both enticing and unsettling. We are hardly surprised when Chandler describes the path leading to a strange, domed hothouse beyond the lawn as 'red flagged'. Marlowe is shown into a glass vestibule 'like a warm oven', and the door is

closed behind him. The butler opens another door and he is hit by a blast of heat.

Inside, the air is thick and wet, 'larded' with the claustrophobic odour of tropical orchids. The glass is heavy with condensation, great drops of water splash from the roof. The light has an 'unreal, greenish colour' as though filtered through an aquarium, the plants like a forest, with 'nasty, meaty leaves'. To Marlowe, a man of the city, they smell as 'overpowering as boiling alcohol under a blanket', a disturbing description.

It does not need to be fathomed. Raymond Chandler deals in atmosphere, not police procedural facts. Few readers will have ever boiled alcohol under a blanket, but we know exactly how Marlowe feels in this steaming glass prison cell. As he is led through the rainforest, trying not to get 'smacked in the face by sodden leaves', he is as vulnerable as most of his clients would be in a barroom shootout.

The butler disappears through the 'abominable plants' leaving Marlowe alone with a strange, unhealthy creature lurking in the jungle clearing. An old, obviously dying man in a wheelchair, his face a 'leaden mask', his lips bloodless, his hands clawlike, stares at the gumshoe with beady black eyes. A few locks of dry hair cling to his scalp 'like wild flowers fighting for life on a bare rock'. The intense smell and dense humidity are overpowering.

'Do you like orchids?' asks the general.

Having allowed ourselves to be led with Marlowe into this sinister, alien greenhouse, we get the distinct feeling that Raymond Chandler

He is beginning to think that the seemingly conflicting universes of suburban greenhouse-dwellers and LA lowlifes are not so very far apart

did not care for orchids. His descriptions, while vivid, are too inaccurate – those 'stalks, like the newly washed fingers of dead men' are probably aerial roots – for a true orchardist. Born in Chicago, educated in London, Chandler would, like his private eye, find his home in the dark underbelly of Los Angeles; there seems to have been no time or place in his life where gardening could have thrived. Although an English Heritage blue plaque has recently been unveiled to him in Upper Norwood, south London, he lived in the Victorian villa for just a few years while studying for exams at Dulwich College. He hated working for the Civil Service, so became a news reporter, but only found his true metier later, in the tough American west coast crime fiction of 1930s pulp novels. It is a fair hunch that Chandler found hothouses as suffocating as his most famous creation does.

'Not particularly,' Marlowe replies to his client's orchid query.

'They are nasty things,' agrees Sternwood, 'their flesh is too much like the flesh of men and their perfume has the rotten sweetness of a prostitute'. The old man admits he exists 'largely on heat, like a newborn spider'. His glass cage is merely an excuse to envelope himself in steam.

Marlowe is more used to enveloping himself in the steam of blondes and brunettes. The heat he understands best is packed by hoodlums, but he is beginning to think that the seemingly conflicting universes of suburban greenhouse-dwellers and LA lowlifes are not so very far apart. Sweating 'like a New England boiled dinner', he gets down to business. The general is being blackmailed; he needs a man who understands such matters. At last, *this* is Marlowe's world.

The orchid house will not appear again in *The Big Sleep*, but its putrid stench will pervade the entire novel. Once more breathing relatively fresh air, Marlowe lights a cigarette and gazes across the Sternwoods' terraces, flowerbeds and trimmed trees, past the high iron fence with its gilded spears, to the source of the family's wealth. Most of the old derricks in the distant oilfield have been removed for a public park, but some still crank darkly, adding more money to already bulging coffers. The family have long since moved uphill, away from the smell.

While Chandler does not often use plants as ciphers, when he does, it is always as shorthand. Streets may be assessed by the trees that line them: pepper trees, eucalyptus trees (which always looks dusty, even after rain), or sometimes nothing at all.

A suspicious character deposits a parcel containing a book, very much of the steamy variety, being part of a pornographic library racket. A storm is brewing: the atmosphere is 'as still as the air in General Sternwood's orchid house'. Marlowe tails the man to a house whose door is entirely concealed by hedge and, on hearing a gunshot, breaks in via the window. 'Neither of the two people in the room paid any attention to the way I came in although only one of them was dead'.

The following day, we can tell our blackmailer has been symbolically washed away by the state of the leaves on Laverne Terrace: they are fresh and green after the rain, but it all seems 'too easy'. His death is only the top layer of a rotten cake. As the investigation deepens, gardens and plants continue to whisper about the humans they represent. The grounds of

Taggart Wilde, DA, are – seemingly – open, with their couple of acres of rolling lawn, but behind the French doors lies a dark garden, mysterious trees and the pervading smell of wet earth and flowers. The Cypress Club, named for its thick grove of Monterey cypress trees, is wreathed in fog. There are few clues to be found here, but this is the City of Angels, *any* mention of green is worth noting. The green-eyed, thigh-swinging ash blonde. The hatless man with the green leather raincoat. The pale green rough wool dress, of the pull-on type, *wink, wink*. The low-cut dress of dull green velvet. The wide hallway with the green carpet. The mean wallpaper with its bright green pine trees. The dame whose eyes narrow until they are a faint green glitter.

There is no greenery, of course, in Marlowe's room, but his unease with plants is well-founded when he arrives home to find a wise guy with a shooter waiting behind the potted palm in his apartment block lobby.

For all his tough-guy talk, Marlowe is always couched as a hero. Slugged by a local hood, he collapses into 'darkness and emptiness, and a rushing wind and a falling as of great trees', a mighty oak felled with a roll of wrapped nickels.

# Behind the French doors lies a dark garden, mysterious trees and the pervading smell of wet earth and flowers

Alongside the wisecracks and one-liners, *The Big Sleep* is most famous for its lack of narrative cohesion. Even Chandler admitted that not all the loose ends are tied, but for him, the most important aspects of a story are its characters and its feel. Given such rough-diamond poetry, it seems prosaic to ask what *really* happened.

In daylight, the Sternwoods' ornamental trees are filled with birds 'crazy with song', their lawns are 'as green as the Irish flag', but the general is no longer making a pretence at life. We are shown into his bedroom not the hothouse. His black eyes remain full of fight but the rest of him looks 'more like a dead man than most dead men look'. The stench of orchids has been replaced by the equally cloying 'sweetish smell of old age'.

Philip Marlowe returns to his car. Later, he will stop at a bar for a couple of double scotches. They won't do him any good. Those gardens 'had a haunted look as though small, wild eyes were watching me from the bushes'. Or maybe they were somewhere else. He is no longer sure. What does it matter where you lie when you're sleeping the Big Sleep?

# The Manor House, Woolton

## *The Importance of Being Earnest*
Oscar Wilde, 1895

*'Oh, flowers are common here, Miss Fairfax, as people are in London'*

Oscar Wilde once told his friend, journalist Robert Ross, that 'we should treat all trivial things in life very seriously, and all serious things of life with a sincere and studied triviality'. On opening in 1895, at the St James Theatre in London's West End, some critics complained that, while intensely witty, there was no 'heart' to *The Importance of Being Earnest*, that there was no 'social message'. They had, of course, missed the point. The very triviality of the dialogue and, indeed, the plot, aimed straight for the heart of Victorian conformity, something for which Wilde himself never had much time.

The play begins in the heart of the city, the Mayfair apartment of Algernon Moncrieff, both urban and urbane, the very opposite of anything 'natural'. Wilde's description tells us the bachelor pad is 'luxuriously and artistically furnished'; this is the world of the crystal-cut upper class. When Algernon asks his friend Jack Worthing where he has been since Thursday, he is shocked at the response: the country. 'What on earth do you do there?' he asks. His friend gloomily replies that 'when one is in town one amuses oneself, when one is in the country one amuses other people'. He confesses the whole thing is a bore.

Wilde himself was in the country when he began the play – or at least the seaside. He spent the summer of 1894 at a villa on the Esplanade

terrace, Worthing, ostensibly allowing his sons a holiday, but in reality needing somewhere to get himself out of a financial hole by writing a hit play. More pressing, he had to get away from constant harassment by the Marquess of Queensbury, who was furious at Wilde's relationship with his son, Lord Alfred Douglas. It seems Wilde had a similar attitude to the seaside as his characters have to the country, describing Worthing as having beautiful surroundings and lovely long walks, 'which I recommend to other people but do not take myself'.

Yet there are compensations to the country, and here a major theme of the play – identity confusion – begins. Both Jack and Algernon have invented excuses to allow themselves a freedom that even upper-class gentlemen would not normally enjoy. Jack has invented 'Ernest', a dissolute brother who needs regular admonishment in town. 'Bunburying', Algernon's practice of disappearing to the country to visit a fictitious invalid called Bunbury, has become part of the English language. Many have suggested that it represented the lot of the homosexual community in Victorian Britain, forced to find their own means of expression in a repressive society.

There is nothing natural in the city. Even afternoon tea is curtailed when no cucumbers may be bought for the sandwiches – 'not even for ready money' (a sly dig at a class floating on a cushion of unsettled merchant credit). As Jack Worthing tries to persuade Lady Bracknell that he is good husband material for her daughter, therefore, he is forced to wax lyrical about the country. He has a country house, he tells her, with

Act Two's setting is – to a nineteenth-century audience at least – the polar opposite of Act One's urban interior

fifteen hundred acres. Lady Bracknell likes the idea of distant wealth, especially in the fashionable home county of Hertfordshire, but like the young men, does not like the idea of actually living there. 'A girl with a simple unspoiled nature like Gwendolen,' she announces, 'could hardly be expected to live in the country'.

Act Two's setting is – to a nineteenth-century audience at least – the polar opposite of Act One's urban interior. While in some respects, he has brought the indoors outside – Wilde specifies basket chairs, a table and books – he is clear it must be a garden. His stage directions demand it should be 'old fashioned'. This description is not completely clear as, by the 1890s, 'old fashioned' may well have meant the classic Victorian formality of carpet bedding and ribbon borders. Wilde clearly does not mean this – he speaks of its being 'full of roses', and including a yew tree and (nonspecific) flowers, watered by Cecily, Jack's niece.

The horticultural equivalent of the Arts and Crafts movement, William Robinson's 'wild gardening' lionized a simpler, blowsier planting system more akin to what it appears Wilde is referring to. People who embraced the style liked to imagine a distant arcadia before the rigours of formality. By 1895, however, it was nearly 25 years old and had heavily seeped into the mainstream, thus Wilde's 'old fashioned' garden may have been, in fact, perfectly fashionable. Not that he would have cared much, Oscar Wilde was many great things but he was no gardener.

It does not seem that his instructions were followed to the letter for the play's first outing. In a sketch that was made for *The Illustrated Sporting*

## He is happy to use gardening as another way of poking at social niceties

*and Dramatic News*, 23 February 1895, the grey stone steps leading to a (distinctly gothic-looking) house are present, but there seem to be fewer flowers than directed, especially roses, and the 'yew' tree looks suspiciously like a beech. Instead of basket chairs, straight bamboo has been chosen, and afternoon tea is set on a matching bamboo table – very much in the current art nouveau style. It is doubtful that Wilde cared; in his descriptions he is aiming for an impression, not horticultural (or garden furnishing) accuracy.

He is happy to use gardening as another way of poking at social niceties, however. Cecily's governess Miss Prism is horrified at her charge's watering the flowers – surely such a 'utilitarian' occupation is the gardener's duty? It is possible that Cecily merely sees the watering as preferable to her schoolwork, but she does have some horticultural knowledge. When she offers to cut a buttonhole for 'Ernest' (a bunburying Algernon) she names the variety of rose with confidence.

'Maréchal Niel' is a genuine climbing rose, but it is unlikely Wilde chose it for Adolphe Niel, the French army general it was named for. The rose is yellow, an extremely popular colour in the 1890s among radicals and intellectuals. It was already associated with the first wave feminist New Woman ideal, but it was also rapidly becoming the colour of decadence, of aesthetes and the underground world of homosexuality.

'No,' replies the definitively heterosexual Algernon, 'I'd sooner have a pink rose'. Pink was for boys, the colour of masculinity. While grown up in stature, Algernon's immaturity does not yet aspire to the more manly,

military red. Yet pink – and roses – also speak of innocence and purity, so Algernon's speedy recovery from an apparently rude refusal of the yellow flower hits the spot when he simperingly compares his Cecily to a pink rose.

Miss Prism has Algernon's number. 'Maturity can always be depended on,' she sniffs. 'Ripeness can be trusted. Young women are green'. She reacts touchily to the sniggers of her audience: 'I spoke horticulturally. My metaphor was drawn from fruit', which somehow renders her words even funnier.

*The Importance of Being Earnest* debuted 14 February 1895 to rapturous acclaim. Light and sweet as meringue, it was just as easily crushed. Wilde, sporting his trademark green carnation (a not-so-secret symbol of his homosexuality for those in the know) was triumphant, having been tipped off and prevented a potential sabotage attempt. The Marquess of Queensbury was stopped at the stage door by constables and was thus unable to throw his bouquet of rotten vegetables at the playwright's feet for having 'corrupted' his son, but he wanted the last, moustache-twirling, cackling laugh.

Fifteen weeks after that triumphant opening night, Wilde was imprisoned for sodomy. Despite its huge popularity, his satirical confection of triviality could not survive such negative publicity and it closed. He would never write another comedy or, indeed, another play. Since then, however, this knickerbocker glory of manners has been revived countless times. It has been celebrated in film, opera, musicals, radio and television; pastiched, translated and adapted to satirize any number of world versions of high society. Above all, it has become profoundly loved, and subsequent productions have taken Wilde's second act instructions for 'an old-fashioned garden' to heart, using the blousy, late Victorian 'wild gardening' style as a metaphor for all things *belle epoque*. The Manor House garden, 'full of roses', whatever their colour, has been welcomed into the theatrical canon. Perhaps Wilde does have the last laugh after all, an open, joyful belly laugh at the trite niceties of a world that rejected him.

# The 'Blue' Gardens

## *The Great Gatsby*
## F. Scott Fitzgerald, 1925

*'Reach me a rose, Honey, and pour me a last drop into that there crystal glass'*

Set in the heady days of a Long Island summer, *The Great Gatsby* is the distilled essence of the Roaring Twenties stereotype: decadence and devil-may-care, bootleg liquor and the Black Bottom dance. Yet F. Scott Fitzgerald never lets us forget that the 1920s was also the era of the blues. An existential melancholy that had begun in the 1860s among impoverished African Americans had, by the end of the First World War, spread throughout a battered nation. Even the wealthy had lost someone or something in the Great War and bright young things seemed to realize they were living on borrowed time. The answer – for an infinitely small elite – was the very opposite of the blues: the red-hot Jazz Age.

The 'blue gardens' is not an official name; it is a description, used only once in the whole novel yet so loaded that it has somehow *become* a name. The grounds of Jay Gatsby's bloated mansion on the wrong side of Long Island are an indigo phantasm of shadows and fleeting mentions; a mysterious world of dark-dappled lawns and rose-perfumed flower beds. Plants are largely inconsequential, however, in this hollow party-land, a mere backdrop to a constantly changing, slow-moving carnival of desperate silhouettes. Gatsby revels in the non-green possibilities of his gardens; the chinking glasses, the swimming pool and the great canvas

## Gardens are commodities to Gatsby, to be bought to facilitate a lifestyle rather than to be enjoyed for themselves

cloth lain across the lawn as a temporary dancefloor for the music that floats across to his next-door neighbour's rather less flashy abode.

Nick Carraway claims never to have liked Gatsby, but he admits curiosity from the start. He has moved to West Egg in time for 'the great burst of leaves growing on the trees, just as things grow in fast movies'. His rented accommodation is small and scruffy but it has a great view across the water to East Egg, where the old money lives.

Fitzgerald's Eggs are based on two real places – the upper-class Sands Point (East Egg) and the nouveau-riche King's Point (West Egg) where Fitzgerald himself moved in 1922. While his own home was not dissimilar to Nick Carraway's, he modelled Gatsby's gaudy fun palace on the great Gold Coast Mansions of the Gilded Age.

An estimated 1,200 lavish country piles were erected along the Long Island North Shore between the 1890s and 1930s. Two in particular are associated with *The Great Gatsby.* Carraway tells us the Gatsby Mansion was 'a colossal affair by any standard' perhaps judging by omission; he does not say he likes it. We learn it was like 'some Hotel de Ville in Normandy, with a tower on one side, spanking new under a thin beard of raw ivy, a marble swimming pool and more than forty acres of land'. Beacon Towers, on Sands Point, a gigantic neo-gothic/Spanish fantasy of turrets and balconies, fitted the mansion description nicely, but Oheka Castle, aka the Otto Khan Estate seems to be a closer match for the grounds. Built in steel and concrete on an artificial hill in 1905, its French chateau styling included a formal sunken garden, extensive greenhouses, orchards and a golf course.

We can paint only an incomplete picture of Gatsby's imaginary gardens, however, from throwaway comments, for they are never described specifically. Carraway descends steps to the sunken area. He notes some pungent roses. The presence of a snub-nose motorboat implies at least part of the estate is accessible by water. The only feature constantly mentioned is Gatsby's lawn. By the 1920s, 'classic' striped lawns were more attainable than ever thanks to the motor mower, capable of cutting up to four acres per day, allowing the possibilities of expanse. Gardens are commodities to Gatsby, to be bought to facilitate a lifestyle rather than to be enjoyed for themselves: 'In his blue gardens men and girls came and went like moths among the whisperings and the champagne and the stars,' writes Fitzgerald.

It is an idyllic thought – until the next morning when we see the servants, armed with mops and scrubbing brushes and garden shears, 'repairing the ravages of the night before'. Someone else does the hard work in this universe.

It does not appear that Fitzgerald was any more interested in gardening than his characters, though he liked gardens if they came with a house suited to his lifestyle. Born to a middle-class family in 1896, he enjoyed a financially up-and-down, playboy lifestyle. By the time he wrote *Gatsby*, he was living, like many impecunious Americans, in Europe, where life remained glamorous but was considerably cheaper than in Long Island.

He was unembarrassed by this. The year he sailed, 1924, he wrote an essay, 'How to Live on Practically Nothing a Year'. It was all relative. The villa he and his wife Zelda shared had a large garden with a summerhouse, 'roses for breakfast and a gardener who called me milord'. Fitzgerald's Jay Gatsby may have been born in New York State, but he came to life on the French Riviera.

At least once a fortnight Gatsby's garden is turned by a 'corps of caterers' into a 'Christmas tree' of coloured lights, spiced baked hams and 'casual innuendo'. His guests live as though they are in an amusement park, their hair bobbed, their flannels pressed, their laughter 'easier minute by minute'. Carraway notes wryly that he was 'one of the few guests who had actually been invited'. This brittle, nocturnal Babylon is so wreathed in shadow that it comes as something of a shock when we next see the garden: in broad daylight, on a Sunday morning. The hedonism continues. One young lady speculates that Gatsby is a murderous bootlegger 'somewhere between his cocktails and his flowers', but somehow the party's host is even more enigmatic in bright sunshine than he was in the darkness.

One of the few times that we get closer to the garden is, perhaps coincidentally, one of the few times we draw closer to Gatsby himself. Uncharacteristically desperate to impress Daisy Buchanan, he declares he wants to cut the grass. He means Carraway's grass, which is long and shaggy in comparison to his own. A man with a raincoat and a lawnmower shows up the next day as Gatsby's drive to control spills from nature to neighbours.

Gatsby apparently derives no personal pleasure from his gardens. It is only through Daisy that he can he enjoy 'the sparkling odour of jonquils and the frothy odour of hawthorn and plum blossoms and the pale gold odour of kiss-me-at-the-gate' (this last is a common name for honeysuckle). All of these flowers seem, perhaps like Gatsby himself, out of place here.

These are semi-wild plants, more at home in the hedgerow or a cottage garden than a Gilded Age hothouse. 'If it wasn't for the mist,' Gatsby tells Daisy, 'we could see your home across the bay'. Across the bay, that is, on the respectable side of Long Island, the part that has always eluded him.

The last time we see Gatsby, he is disappearing into 'yellowing trees'. The summer is over. In the swimming pool a cluster of fallen leaves revolves in the breeze on the surface of the water, tracing a thin circle of red. The contaminated grass is merely that – grass – no longer a lawn. Carraway tells us that that 'when the blue smoke of brittle leaves was in the air' he headed back home to the west, because now the east was haunted. The reader might beg to disagree. It was always haunted.

Eternal blue mists drift in and out of Gatsby's gardens like the 'sparkling hundreds' constantly moving, ghost-like, through the shadows. Another tune begins, another bottle is opened, another cocktail mixed. Everything seems distant, as though viewed through the wrong end of a telescope or heard through the scratchy shellac grooves of a gramophone record.

Perhaps it is better like that. Specifics would break the spell.

# Visiting

By their very nature, not all of the gardens in this book are visitable, though some may be 'experienced' through the authors' homes or places that inspired their gardens. Here are some suggestions:

**Alice's Adventures in Wonderland**
Christ Church Gardens and Christ Church Meadow in Oxford are semi-public spaces, some of which may be visited by the public.
*chch.ox.ac.uk/visit/gardens*

**The Black Tulip**
Loevestein Castle is open to the public, but to fully understand the historical draw of the tulip, a visit to the Black Tulip Museum in Lisse is highly recommended.
*slotloevestein.nl/en/a-day-at-loevestein*
*museumdezwartetulp.nl*

**The Chronicles of Narnia**
C.S. Lewis's home The Kilns may be visited by appointment only. Cair Paravel was also inspired by the ruined Dunluce Castle in Northern Ireland.
*cslewis.org/ourprograms/thekilns/kilnstour*
*discovernorthernireland.com/things-to-do/dunluce-castle*

**The Garden of the Finzi-Continis**
Many Bassani fans are disappointed each year when they turn up in Ferrara hoping to find his imaginary park. They would be far better served visiting the extraordinary gardens at Ninfa, in Latina, central Italy.
*giardinodininfa.eu*

**'The Garden Party'**
Katherine Mansfield's house and garden in Wellington, New Zealand, an inspiration for the Sheridan Garden, is open to the public Tuesdays to Sundays.
*katherinemansfield.com*

**The Great Gatsby**
Beacon Towers, one of the mansions associated with *The Great Gatsby*, was demolished in 1945, but Oheka Castle is now a hotel.
*oheka.com*

**'Kew Gardens'**
The Royal Botanic Gardens, Kew, is a few minutes' walk from Kew Gardens underground station, west London. It is open daily, save for Christmas Day.
*kew.org/kew-gardens*

**Larry's Party**
All of Larry's mazes in *Larry's Party* are fictional, but the English mazes at Hampton Court Palace and Saffron Walden that first inspire him, are accessible to visit.
*hrp.org.uk/hampton-court-palace*
*visitsaffronwalden.gov.uk*

**My Mother's House *and* Sido**
In 2011 the Association La Maison de Colette purchased Colette's childhood home. Five years later, it was opened to the public for guided tours. There are also suggested Colette walks around the town of La Puisaye, including the Colette Museum, in a local chateau.
*www.maisondecolette.fr*

**The Pillow Book**
Very little remains of original Heian period Japanese gardens, but To-in Teien (East Palace Garden) has been recently recreated from archaeological excavations at Nara Palace Site Historical Park, and is thought to be similar to those enjoyed by Sei Shōnagon.
*heijo-park.jp/en/area/fukugen*

**Rāmāyaṇa**
The *Rāmāyaṇa* is so very ancient that many sites are associated with events and characters in its verses. One of the most famous is the Sita Amman Temple, Sri Lanka, seven kilometres southeast of Nuwara Eliya.

**'Rappaccini's Daughter'**
It is unlikely anyone would want to visit the poison-filled garden of the imaginary Dr Rappaccini, but it is very clearly modelled on the nearby Orto Botanico 1545, the world's oldest university Botanical Garden, open to the public through much of the year.
*ortobotanicopd.it/en*

**Rebecca**
Daphne du Maurier's home Menabilly is private, but three cottages on the grounds of her former Cornish estate are let as holiday homes.
*menabilly.com*

**The Secret Garden**
Despite Misselthwaite Manor's supposed situation on the Yorkshire moors, Frances Hodgson Burnett's home, Great Maytham Hall in Kent, is most associated with *The Secret Garden*. It is occasionally open to visitors via the National Gardens Scheme (NGS).
*ngs.org.uk/great-maytham-hall-kent-the-most-famous-garden-in-literature*

**The Tale of Peter Rabbit**
While Beatrix Potter's garden at Hill Top was not made until after *The Tale of Peter Rabbit* was written, it is likely she made it with Mr McGregor in mind. The walled garden at Gwaenynog, Wales, was another of her inspirations, though mainly for another book, *The Tale of the Flopsy Bunnies*. It is open occasionally for the National Gardens Scheme (NGS).
*nationaltrust.org.uk/visit/lake-district/hill-topngs.org.uk*

# About the Author & Illustrator

**Sandra Lawrence**

Sandra Lawrence has written for all the broadsheets and many magazines, as well as over 20 books, including *Lost Gardens* (Frances Lincoln), *Miss Willmott's Ghosts* (Bonnier) and *The Witch's Garden* series for The Royal Botanic Gardens, Kew/Welbeck: *The Witch's Garden*; *The Magic of Mushrooms*; *The Witch's Forest*; *The Psychedelic Garden*). For children, she is the author of the *Atlas* series (*Atlas of Beasts; Atlas of Heroes*), *Anthology of Amazing Women* (Templar) and *A Magical Guide to Plants* (Royal Botanic Gardens, Kew and Welbeck).

**Lucille Clerc**

Lucille Clerc is a French illustrator. She mainly works in editorial, installations and murals. Her favourite themes are the city and Nature and their sometimes symbiotic, sometimes antagonistic relationships. She develops these subjects in opulent narrative compositions filled with a myriad of decorative and architectural details, observed on site, that the viewer explores like a territory.

# Index

Quarto

First published in 2025 by Frances Lincoln,
an imprint of The Quarto Group.
One Triptych Place, London, SE1 9SH,
United Kingdom
T (0)20 7700 9000 / www.Quarto.com

EEA Representation, WTS Tax d.o.o., Žanova ulica 3,
4000 Kranj, Slovenia
www.wts-tax.si



A catalogue record for this book is available from the British Library.

ISBN 978-1-8360-0220-8
Ebook ISBN 978-1-8360-0221-5

10 9 8 7 6 5 4 3 2 1

Design by Eleanor Ridsdale Colussi

Publisher: Philip Cooper
Senior Commissioning Editor: Alice Graham
Editor: Katerina Menhennet
Editorial Assistant: Izzy Toner
Senior Designer: Isabel Eeles
Production Controller: Rohana Yusof

Printed in Huizhou, Guangdong, China TT/Jun/25